GW00702017

# How Twins Grow Up

# How Twins Grow Up

## Mary Rosambeau

THE BODLEY HEAD
LONDON

For my friend Jenny Hills

British Library Cataloguing in Publication Data

Rosambeau, Mary
How twins grow up
1. Twins
I. Title
305.9′045 QL 971

ISBN 0 370 31090 X
© Mary Rosambeau 1987

Printed and bound in Great Britain for
The Bodley Head Ltd
32 Bedford Square, London WC1B 3EL
by
St Edmundsbury Press Ltd,
Bury St Edmunds, Suffolk

*First published 1987*

# Contents

## Part I
### What can science tell us about twins?

## Part II
### What do twins themselves have to say?

# PART I

# *What can science tell us about twins?*

# CHAPTER 1

# *Why do we need a book on twins?*

One out of every fifty people in the United Kingdom is born a twin. If on a crowded double decker bus one were to shout, "Is anyone here a twin?" the likelihood is that at least one person would answer "Yes". Before effective contraception made smaller families possible there were even more twins with about one pair being born in every eighty births.

Most of us can recall at least one set of twins from among our acquaintances. Perhaps there were twins at school with us; maybe we can remember a pair who were occasionally seen around the town where we grew up. Twins whom we notice tend to be of the 'look alike' or the 'identical' kind so that when we learn that these account for only a third of all twins born in Britain we begin to appreciate just how widespread twinship is.

Once parents put away their twin prams however there is little left to indicate that this non-identical majority of paired children are twins. An occasional joint birthday, or the fact that they start school together, will jog the memory but they themselves show little visible evidence of their twinship. We however still find ourselves wondering whether having grown up in such close partnership may not have affected each individual personality in some subconscious way.

Society adopts a specific attitude to twins. Because of this even twins themselves are led to expect that they should feel especially close to each other. But is there a mystical bond between twins? If a pair do become very close does this mean that they cut themselves off from others, or does the close proximity in which they have been brought up help them to be more sociable? Does their shared experience allow them to draw strength from each other or does it merely mean more quarrels? Are both equally affected by their pairing or does one always take the lead and the other follow? The subject of twinship raises all sorts of questions and although the discussion is a fascinating one it rarely provides us with answers.

The spaced brothers and sisters in a family may also choose to form close ties, exclude others, or make dominant dependent relationships with each other, but because of their special situation twins tend to be thrown together quite irrespective of their personal choice. Few pre-school twins have ever known an environment which did not contain their twin. Mother will kiss each one goodnight and leave the room but one's twin will still be there. He will still be there next morning to be washed with you, dressed with you, and during the day, whether cuddling you or kicking you there he will be right next to you sharing your pram.

Unlike even the closest siblings this shared twin life goes right back to the point of conception. As they develop in the womb even the physical position each takes up to prepare for birth is dictated by how the other lies. It may not be too fanciful to suggest that the later psychological positions twins may adopt may also be influenced by the constant proximity in which they spend their first formative years.

Whether we think that twins affect each other's attitude or not we already know that as a pair they undoubtedly have an effect on us. Twins elicit one of two responses from almost everyone they meet; they are either subjected to constant comparison or else treated as though they were a single unit. No one seems to be clear about the effect of this on the individuals concerned. Does comparison undermine their confidence? Might being treated as a pair inhibit their individual development? At every turn thinking about twins seems to pose us with questions.

Twinship however is only one aspect of the total personal attributes of any one twin. The questions we have been looking at can only be considered in the context of each individual case. Being a twin is however fairly significant, and any assessment which totally ignores this cannot pretend to be giving a full picture of the person concerned.

There are practical situations where our ignorance of the influence of twinship can make our every-day decisions more difficult. For example, a decision to teach twins in different classes is often delayed because teachers and parents are vague about the effect such a separation will have on the children concerned. On wider issues the general dictum that being fair to children cannot be wrong may need re-examination where twins are concerned. To treat twins in exactly the same way may mean that we fail them as individuals. Indecision as to how important twinship is for boy/girl pairs can also interfere with our judgement so that it is either ignored altogether or else they are treated as a unisex pair for far too long.

As a parent of twins myself, I searched for the answers to these and other questions when my pair were young. I wanted to make the best decisions for them and so I tried to read widely on the subject. I was surprised to draw a blank. I found twin carburettors and twin-engined bombers in the library index but no one seemed to have anthing to say about human twins. Scientific journals did tell me about their biological origin and whether or not they had shared a placenta, but although it made fascinating reading it was not what I wanted to know. I needed help to handle the fact that as toddlers no incident seemed to occur when my treatment of one did not affect what was felt by the other. I wanted suggestions for the future. How should I cope if as teenagers one turned out to be more popular than the other? I also wanted someone to tell me whether my concentration on their twinship was just a lot of fuss or whether their being twins was in fact something extra to their being just my daughters.

To my surprise I discovered that it was not only parents who wanted this sort of information but that many adults who were twins themselves were also on this quest.

"I read everything I can lay my hands on about twins," said one lady of seventy, showing me her vast collection of cuttings. And why not? After all, most of us are fascinated by our beginnings, by our family history, and by anything that might throw light on what has shaped us into the people we now are.

Talking to these adult twins I found that some had amusing memories of the effect their twinship had had on their parents.

"Our mother concentrated on treating us the same to the point that if my twin had pink pudding then I had to have pink pudding too, no matter that I didn't like the ruddy stuff!" laughed a lawyer.

But others, on a more serious note, helped to confirm my growing conviction that a wider understanding of twinship was needed if young people were not to be mishandled merely because they were twins.

"I was one of these victims who passed exams where my sister failed, so my parents felt it would not be fair for one to go to grammar school and the other not, so I did not get the opportunity of further education. I only discovered this many years afterwards and felt very bitter about it," said one lady who had spent many years later in life taking her 'O' and 'A' levels at evening classes in order to train as the teacher she had always wanted to be.

How many other decisions are made for twins by well meaning people blinded by the fact that they are dealing with a pair? If this sort of misunderstanding is widespread, teachers, parents and twins themselves ought to be informed.

This book will not deal with bizarre or insurmountable problems but with those areas where a little extra knowledge may be enough to change attitudes in a small way, but may also have a major effect on the management of children who are twins. At first we need to get our facts right, so we look at what scientists can tell us about twins. The conception and the birth of twin babies has intrigued men for centuries and a lot has been learned. Once they were born however scientific interest in twins tended to diminish, and in order to discover what actually happens to children when they grow up as a pair we have had to turn to the twins themselves and to the parents who have watched them grow.

The patterns which emerged from the remembered experience of 600 twins and the parents of twins form the second part of the book and go some way towards suggesting answers to the sort of questions we have been asking. But, like all good surveys, this one has also uncovered some unexpected additional areas of interest which deepen the understanding of twinship in other ways as well.

# CHAPTER 2

# A subject of mystery and myth

## Twins in other cultures

In the past Japanese nobility were ashamed to admit that twins had been born into their families. It was felt that only the lower animals gave birth to litters. The fact of their twinship would be hidden or one of the children would be given away. A worse fate awaited twins born in other countries. Among peoples as far apart as the eskimo at the North Pole and the Australian aborigine of the southern hemisphere, it was the custom to kill one or both twins at birth. Superstititions and fears of evil portents surrounded these customs, but it is quite possible that they grew up out of practical necessity. If a tribe were nomadic the mother carrying two infants might become a burden; if it was pastoral depending on every member doing his or her share in the fields a woman might manage with one baby on her back but be seriously hampered when caring for two.

In Africa, however, tribes of the same social and economic structure and occupying adjacent territories could be found to hold totally opposing views with regard to the birth of twins. In the one, their arrival would be greeted as a sign of good fortune, and in the other it would be seen as an omen of evil. Practical explanations did not seem to apply here. In fact the omens and portents were not seen as referring to the family of the twins alone but as extending to embrace the tribe as a whole.

Where twins were welcome they were expected to fulfil a special role in the tribal rituals and were regarded with respect throughout their lives. Their mother was also highly honoured. Among the kaffirs of southern Africa, for example, she was the only woman allowed to sit with the men at social gatherings.

Where twins were feared the infants were often taken out into the jungle and abandoned. Mary Slessor, a Scottish missionary who went to Africa at the turn of the century, founded an orphanage on her mission station for the abandoned twins of the surrounding tribes. In some cases the ritual of the tribe demanded the death of the twins and sometimes that of the mother also. Where she was spared she was regarded as having been tainted and was excluded from the tribe altogether. In areas where this has been the practice in the recent past, "May you become the mother of twins!" is still held to be a very potent curse.

The favourable attitude to the arrival of twin babies can be understood in terms of the tribe's approval of the mother's fertility and the hope that it might also extend to the tribe's other activities. The rituals in which twins were expected to take part were associated with the planting of crops, praying for rain, and also attendance at weddings. The killing of twins on the other hand, and especially the killing of the mother, may have stemmed from the suspicion that the birth of two children at the same time was a tangible proof that the mother had had intercourse with two different males. A closer look at what was actually believed, however, shows that these killings were not done as a simple punishment for adultery but out of fear that one of the males might have been the devil himself.

Even serious studies applying common-sense methods to the study of twins frequently come up against similar implications of involvement with the supernatural.

All down the centuries twins have been associated with myths and magic. This is one of the reasons why it is now so difficult to tease out which of our current attitudes are based on reason and which on old wives' tales. In our own time, extrasensory perception, perhaps the nearest thing to magic in our scientific age, is the first thing some people will think of when twins are mentioned.

Attitudes from earlier times and from other cultures still echo in our society. Twins were often then regarded as belonging to the tribe and their immediate families were seen to be almost irrelevant. We do not worship the sun or pray to the moon but schools and other institutions frequently refer to 'our' twins, gossiping neighbours see themselves as expressing the judgement of the whole community when they express criticism of the way that twins are being brought up.

A young mother wrote recently from her village:
"There are many people who have been quite hostile to us over

the way we are bringing up our daughters—we feel they should be treated like individuals. Some people think this is a disgrace. They also say that because they are identical we should be dressing them alike. Would they behave in the same way to parents whose children were a couple of years apart?"

These external social attitudes often exert a tangible pressure on those of us who are parents of twins. What makes this doubly difficult for us, however, is that we too are members of the society which holds these views. This makes for an element of confusion between our particular knowledge of our own children as individuals and our normal share in the common view held about twins in general. Harassed parents of pre-school twins are often puzzled to hear themselves give the "Twins how nice!" response when they meet other parents with another young pair. They of all people, they feel, should know that 'nice' is the last word which appropriately describes life with twins when they are tiny. And yet the spontaneous sentimental response slips out. Its origins must lie very far back in our primitive past not to have been overtaken by our more recently acquired experience.

## Twins in Mythology

If we trace back into antiquity we can find very definite expressions of commonly held views on twins. Ancient lore was not only responsible for perpetuating superstition but also for preserving and handing down a great deal of human wisdom. Tellers of tales in the oral tradition soon sifted out the truth from the trivia in their stories. From the audience response they could judge which characters were believable and which motives in their plots rang true. The tales which survived were very often based on the same familiar domestic crises which were well known then and are still our common experience today.

The story of the founding of Rome tells of Romulus and Remus, twin brothers abandoned and brought up by a she-wolf. They became mighty warriors but quarrelled as adults over the site where they should build their new city of Rome. The ensuing fight was so bitter that Romulus killed Remus, even though he was his twin. Another story tells of Narcissus who, longing for his dead twin sister, spent his time gazing at his reflection in pools so that he might be reminded of her. Even today we can recognise in these tales the closeness of some twins who are drawn together, and also the state of rivalry which can exist between others which seems to push them apart.

### Twins as a totem in society today

In spite of the wide-ranging insight of the ancients, and in this case, in spite of their appreciation of the psychology of twins, our modern perception of twinship has concentrated only on one single type. The slight disappointment we feel at the sight of twins who are not alike is proof of this. We really want to be amazed by their similarity. Even those of us who are parents of twins, because we are the products of this same society, go along with this. When asked if my own children are twins I often hear myself reply, "Oh yes, but they are not identical . . ." as though that in some way invalidates their twinship. Parents of non-identical twins who wrote to offer help with background for this book frequently began their letters by saying, "I expect you are only interested in identicals . . ." and even "Although mine are not true twins . . ."

'True twins' is an attractive concept. It conveys a double message: twins who are 'real' in some way, but also twins who are 'true' to each other in the sense of loyalty and friendship, but above all 'true' twins implies twins who are close. A single born adult may remark, "I never got on with my sister . . ." and it is taken as a normal case of sibling rivalry. It may even be answered by a nod of understanding and the reply, "No, neither did I". A twin who says the same thing, however, is taken to be making a more significant statement.

"It has always been one of my greatest regrets that my sister and I are not close and have not been so since our teens. I am sure my twin and I cannot be regarded as normal in that we do not have a close relationship. I have always felt that we missed out . . . I hope there are not too many like us."

Another twin reflects, "I can't remember a time when we were really friends. I'd like to have been."

Both the speakers and we, the listeners, are wistful for what might have been. It seems as though our society expects every twin to do his or her duty as a symbol of closeness. Perhaps this is what is required that they do for the tribe today.

Agricultural fertility is now being looked after by science, and the presence of twins at a wedding to ensure fertility might be an embarrassment to a couple who intend to postpone their family, but the idea of twins still has strong symbolic power.

Today, when human relationships are notoriously shaky and it is difficult for an older generation to pass on a concept of loyalty and mutual concern to serve as a model for the young, romantic love has somehow failed to convey the idea of enduring to the end which the older concept of 'brotherly' love can still imply. Close twins dressed alike, moving in unison and acting as one, perhaps present a living picture of the ideal relationship between two people. Today the totem twins carry for the tribe is the symbol of social harmony, a reminder that this is still a possibility between partners.

Social symbols are so strong that visually we tend to insist that they do conform to the idea they represent. Looking at a bridal party lined up for the wedding photograph we see the white dress as the symbol of virginity it is worn to represent. The bride's mother may be in a state of anxiety in case her careful dressmaking fails to hide the premature swelling of the waistline. But most guests will *want* to see a beautiful bride in a white dress and that is what they will see. The mother need only fear the glance of those close friends who see the bride as herself, the girl they know who happens to be a bride in white for today.

In the same way, people continually insist that they see all twins as identical pairs and go to extraordinary lengths to convince themselves that nonexistent likenesses exist. Where twins are identical any suggestions that they don't get on are brushed aside as mistaken; any stories of pairs who have quarrelled are treated as questionable and the reporter as misinformed.

### The pressure of pairing

Against these insistent pressures of society's expectations, parents of twin children have to make a conscious effort to present and preseve the individuality of each member of their particular pair. Strangely enough, triplets do not seem to attract the pressure to remain in a unit as twins do. Triplet sets can be made up of three quite separate and visually dissimilar children, three visually and genetically identical children, or three children, two of whom are genetically and visually identical, plus one other who does not look like the other two at all. In these sets containing the identical pairs parents find that society offers the "Twins how nice" response to what they think are twins, then "Triplets how amazing!" when they find out that all three are triplets. Almost invariably, however, attention drifts back to the identical pair and curiosity about their closeness tends to dominate the conversation.

"The pair" as a concept seems to have a special significance in the human mind. We find the temptation to regard paired individuals as a single unit very difficult to resist. Twins themselves vouch for this.

"When we were about eight we had to draw out of a hat to see who would crown the statue in May. Some parents said we should only draw once as otherwise it would be like having two turns. They could not see we were two people."

The Guliksen twins who play the international tennis circuits say that they frequently have to fight for the right to have a car each when they go on tour, as other members of the team. It is always assumed that one between them is all that they require despite the fact that they lead separate lives.

This tendency to see twins as a unit may explain the common apprehensions about parting them. One shoe or one glove is no use without the other. Does this perhaps colour what we feel when confronted by only one twin? Outsiders hesitate to separate twins for fear some deep psychological damage may be done, yet equally twins who derive a great deal from each other's company are suspected of being trapped within their relationship. Just like the two African tribes who held opposing views, so two adjacent schools today may be poles apart in their attitudes to twins. In one they will automatically be placed in the same class while in the other no pair will ever be allowed to stay together.

*Professionals too are caught in the same trap*

Just as parents are confused by being part of the society which makes irrational assumptions about twins, so too teachers and other professionals are affected by the attitudes of this society to which they belong. Even the most concerned teacher or doctor is unlikely to have first hand knowledge of more than a handful of twins during his whole career. Health and education policies tend therefore to be based on knowledge of a few cases which is then applied in general to all. Parents hoping for advice and guidance are often puzzled by conflicting opinions or even offended by dogmatic direction. Either way they tend to end up more confused than ever.

*The need for solid factual information*

Well balanced, happy adults emerge from homes where people know exactly where they stand. Confusion leads to uncertainty and uncertainty can make one insecure. If we are to make informed decisions about helping the child who is a twin towards a confident and competent adulthood we need to counter the pressures of society with as many solid facts as we can find. For this reason the first chapters of this book concentrate on the scientific facts about twinning, and on the findings of recent research into the effects of being a twin. From that framework of information we will then be in a better position to appreciate these patterns which emerge in the experience of those who have themselves grown up as twins, which is presented in the second part of this study.

# CHAPTER 3

# Beginning at the beginning

Many common questions about twins can be cleared up by looking at how they come to be born together in the first place. Most of us have some idea about the splitting of the egg, but even this information can give rise to misunderstandings. Only a few years ago one mother wrote:

"I was horrified when this passerby remarked that it was sad to think that such pretty children should have only one lung and one kidney between them." Another had met the same idea somewhere else:

"One Mum at our toddler group suggested that the reason why my twins had such a lot of coughs and colds was that they were each only half a baby."

Biologically twins fall into two groups; mono-zygotic or 'identical', so called because they do tend to look alike: and di-zygotic or 'fraternal' because they tend to resemble each other only as much as other sisters and brothers would do. The 'zygote' in mono-zygotic and di-zygotic is the scientific name for the first development stage of the fertilized egg formed when one sperm combines with one egg to spark off the beginning of another new life.

A zygote is just visible to the naked eye. It contains forty-six microscopic strands called chromosomes, twenty-three of which have come from the mother inside the egg, and twenty-three brought from the father by the sperm. These chromosomes are made up of even tinier particles called genes, which will programme the whole development of this future human being. Eye colour, hair texture, and we now think, even future manner-isms, are dictated by these genes which begin their work within a few hours of conception taking place.

Di-zygotic twins come from two separate zygotes. What is unusual in their case is that the two eggs should be available for fertilization at the same time. In the ordinary way only one egg is released from a woman's ovaries in each monthly cycle. A hormone stimulates the development of eggs, but once one egg has ripened and been shed, another hormone is secreted which inhibits the growth of any more. Where di-zygotic twins are conceived the inhibiting hormone has been slow to take effect so that two are shed before egg development stops. Where twins run in a family, this double ovulation is probably the hereditary factor which is passed down as it is only this di-zygotic type of twin which tends to recur.

Mono-zygotic twins as their name suggests, come from only one zygote which splits in two. All zygotes develop by dividing, but they do this within their outer skin. After fertilization each chromosome doubles in size and then peels apart into two replicas of the original, as though being opened up by zip fasteners. Under the microscope it is possible to see these new strips move away from each other. Like partners in a square dance, each matching half takes up station at opposite sides of the nucleus, then like a balloon which is being tied in the middle, the whole constricts in the centre, the two halves pull apart, and there, still within the outer skin, are two identical copies of the original. Both nuclei now contain an identical set of chromosomes made up of the genes which will control the next, and all subsequent, phases of development.

Zygotes grow by repeating this division of their cells until the whole bundle looks rather like a raspberry. The scientific name for this stage is in fact the murula, or mulberry, which is another fruit with a similar sort of structure. If this were all that happened, babies would end up looking like a mass of frog spawn, so fortunately now a change takes place.

From now on cells differentiate into special groups. Some move away from the centre to form an outer layer called the chorion, others cluster together to form the beginnings of the embryo which is then surrounded by an inner protective layer which will become the amniotic sac.

At any time up to this stage the division which results in mono-zygotic twins can occur. For some, as yet unknown reason, there are times when not only the inner cell mass but the whole zygote divides and pulls apart into two separate entities. As each part still contains its own set of chromosomes necessary to programme future development, so both can con-

## Cells Splitting

showing only three of the forty-six Chromosomes.

1. Each Chromosome doubles in size and peels apart into two replicas of itself.

2. Each matching half takes up station at opposite sides of the nucleus.

3. The whole constricts in the centre, and the two halves begin to pull apart.

4. And there still within the outer skin are two identical copies of the original ready to double and split again.

tinue to grow on as before, only now each will develop into a separate individual.

If this division, or fission, happens before or at the murula stage, the two cell clusters will continue to develop just as though they had originated as two separate zygotes. If it occurs after this first stage however, the outer chorion will have already formed and any future divisions will take place within it. The earliest result of this is two embryos each with its own amniotic sac, surrounded by one outer chorion.

As the placenta, through which the developimg embryos are nourished, develops at the point where the chorion comes in contact with the wall of the mother's womb, this pair of twins will have to share their placenta. Mono-zygotic twins from earlier divisions will each have their own placenta, as do di-zygotic twins, as each embryo is surrounded by its own individual chorion.

Division for some twins comes even later. The embryo may divide after the formation of the amnion so that two babies develop within the same sac. This can be very dangerous as they are not protected from each other's movements, and their umbilical cords may tangle and even knot together. Later divisions are rare, but they can occur even after the umbilical cord has implanted in the placenta, when it forks to supply the two embryos. As we can see, these divisions are getting closer and closer.

A very late division will sometimes be incomplete and the two embryos produced will then remain partly attached to each other. Twins like these are known as conjoined or siamese twins. All these very late divisions are contained within one chorion. They develop within the same amniotic sac and have only one shared placenta.

Conjoined twins are very rare. They occur only about once in a thousand twin births. Nowadays an effort is usually made to separate them soon after they are born, and in cases where only the outer embryonic tissue is involved there is a good chance of success.

The most famous conjoined twins, Chang and Eng Bunker, were born in Siam in 1811, which is why such twins are called siamese. They were joined at the breast bone by a five inch band of cartilage. When they were young this was quite supple, and it

## Identical Twinning

1. Early Division – not only the inner cell mass but the whole zygote divides and pulls apart.

2. Once the chorion has formed all later divisions take place within it.

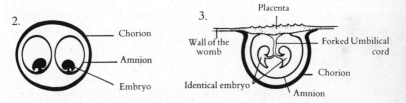

3. Divison can take place even after the zygote implants in the wall of the womb. This is a very late division which can take place after the development of a single umbilical cord.

was possible for one to turn a somersault while the other remained standing still. An American sea captain visiting their village persuaded them to return with him to America, where they travelled with a circus for some years before settling down to become successful farmers. They married two girls who were sisters and between them had twenty-two children. As they grew older one of them developed an uncertain temper, and began to drink heavily. It is thought that his drinking may have contributed to his death at the age of sixty-two. It is generally thought also, that his brother Eng, who survived him by only a few hours, died from shock.

The fact that siamese twins, who of course are mono-zygotic or identical twins, can develop different personalities, comes as a surprise to most people. The sight of two people as alike as two peas in a pod, whose very actions resemble one another, leads one to assume that their thinking and temperament must be similar too. Twins who had been separated at birth and brought up apart from each other did seem to show that this was in fact the case.

In the past if twin babies were offered for adoption, it was common practice to place each one with a different family. Then they grew up in complete ignorance of the fact that they had had a twin. Some however retained a distinct impression that they had at one time been part of a pair, and as adults set out to find their missing partner. Nowadays those who are successful often make headlines, which is when they may be contacted by Professor Thomas J. Bouchard, Director of the Minnesota Center for Twin and Adoption Research, of the USA.

With the change in adoption practice, which makes it very unlikely that anyone will in future separate twin children, there will probably be no more cases of twins who have been brought up apart. Because of this, those who have had that experience present science with a rare opportunity to study the effects of their shared heredity.

Reunited couples are invited to the Institute for tests of all kinds, where it has been proved that the influence of their identical genetic programme has persisted right throughout their lives. Not only are their looks and tastes very similar, but idiosyncrasies which could in no way have been picked up by chance match up uncannily. One pair of male twins discovered that each had the same habit of flushing the toilet both before and after using it. Brothers might have picked this up from a hygiene-conscious mother, but as in their case not a day of their early training had been shared, it would seem that even some of our minor habits are dictated by our genes.

When these reunited pairs were compared for similarity with other sets of mono-zygotic twins who had grown up together however, an interesting fact emerged. Those brought up apart were *more* similar to each other than were those who had spent their lives together.

The key point at which the two sets differed was not so much that their general environment had been similar or different, but that in the case of those brought up together, the environment had always contained their twin.

A twin herself explained how this can work:

"We are very much alike, we walk, talk and think alike. We have the same mannerisms so much so that, when I am with her for a day I feel, when I look at her, it is as if I am looking at myself. It isn't a feeling that I like, because the things I see in her that I know are like myself—I don't like, and I become critical of myself."

Chang and Eng who could not have lived more closely together gradually became less and less like each other too. It is easier to see this process at work in identical twins, but proximity forces fraternal twins to make similar comparisons. Here we see one of the first indications of how twinship may affect the development of children who have shared a single birth.

# CHAPTER 4

# *More facts from science*

Twins come in five different types of pairing: genetically identical girls, genetically identical boys, fraternal boy pairs, fraternal
girl pairs, and the pairs which are made up of one boy and one
girl.

Fathers contribute the chromosome which decides the sex of
their children. A mother's eggs all carry the same sex chromosome, usually referred to as the X chromosome. About half the
father's sperm carry a Y chromosome, which when combined
with the mother's X gives the XY necessary for a baby boy.

In the case of di-zygotic twins the two eggs available for
fertilization may either meet two sperm each carrying an X
chromosome, in which case this will give two XXs for two girls,
or they will meet two sperm each carrying a Y giving the two
XY pairs for two boys. They may also however meet one
carrying an X and one which carries a Y giving the one XX pair
and one XY pair necessary for one boy and one girl.

A single zygote which is later going to split into identical twins
will start off with only one pair of sex chromosomes, either XX
or XY. When it splits it can only divide into two XXs or into two
YYs. This is why identical twins can only ever be of the same sex
and why boy/girl twins will always belong to the non-identical
group.

Sometimes however a family likeness will be strong enough
for even boy/girl twins to look alike. It is possible that William
Shakespeare's own twin son and daughter were of this type as he
used look-alike brother/sister pairs in as many as nine of his
plays. It is in fact much easier to see why mono-zygotic twins
should look alike than why di-zygotic twins should look
different.

Every human being has forty-six chromosomes but each new
egg and each new sperm carries a different combination of the
twenty-three which have been selected from the mother's and

father's forty-six. Mathematicians have worked out that the maximum possible number of different combinations is 64,000,000,000, giving that number of potentially different kinds of children for just one couple.

To complicate things further, chromosomes, when they meet, indulge in something called 'crossing over'. The result of this is that the actual possible number of combinations could end up even higher. In view of this, it is amazing that any children in a family, let alone twins, should show any resemblance to each other at all. For most couples, however, there are some genes which will always win in a choice between brown eyes like mother or blue like dad, or between the large feet of his family and the dainty ones she has. These stronger genes make family likenesses possible but despite them no two zygotes ever contain exactly the same pattern of genes, and this is part of the reason that every child who is born can be regarded as being quite unique.

Just as some di-zygotic twins may look alike, some mono-zygotic pairs may not look absolutely identical. Even sharing a placenta does not always guarantee it will be shared equally so some identical twins will vary in size at birth because of the difference in their nourishment. Experience even in the womb will not necessarily be the same for each embryo even in a mono-zygotic pair, and so the *difference in environment* is the other part of what ensures that even identical twins, with exactly the same genetic structure, are still individually unique.

To qualify as a twin one must have shared the same pregnancy. It is even possible for twin children to have different birthdays, and still be twins. This happens when a pair are born one on either side of midnight. It also happens in rare cases where the womb 'shuts down' after the first baby is born to 'start up again' some time later for the delivery of the second twin. Twin pairs have been delivered as much as twenty days apart. Both infants survived and are still rightly referred to as twins.

In the case of di-zygotic twins who result from two separate eggs, it is usually supposed that they have been fertilized by two sperm from the same ejaculation. It is quite possible, however, for twins to result from two quite separate acts of coition. Two babies can be born after a twin pregnancy showing all the physical signs usually put down to difference in age.

The most convincing proof that twins have been conceived at different times however comes from the courts of law. Several paternity cases have been reported where a blood test on the alleged father has proved that he could have contributed to the conception of only one of the babies. In some cases both fathers have been identified and each has contributed to the maintenance of his particular twin.

These blood tests which are used in paternity cases can also be used to decide the genetic type or 'zygocity' of twins themselves. Blood is made up of about twenty-nine different chemicals, each of which is the direct responsibility of a single set of genes. Blood tests compare the composition of the samples taken from each twin and if it is exactly the same the twins are mono-zygotic or identical twins. If however even one of the twenty-nine constituents is different they must be fraternal or di-zygotic.

Laboratories are busy places and not likely to carry out this complicated test for frivolous reasons. It would be done for example if one twin were in need of a skin graft or an organ transplant. Clear proof that twins were identical would then be welcomed in these cases because the tissue from one mono-zygotic twin can be accepted by the body of the other without all the usual problems of rejection.

Twins themselves, however, would often welcome some definite information about their origin. One twin remembered the relief of having finally discovered that she was not as she had thought 'a mere replica' of her sister. Another pair who belong to the group of 'not so identical' identical twins found particular comfort in the discovery that they really did 'belong' together in this special way.

There are quite a few indicators which even an amateur observer can use to tell that twins are *not* identical. Boy/girl twins, as we have seen, can immediately be diagnosed as di-zygotic. Twins with different eye colours cannot be identical as we know that a single gene controls the colour of the eyes. Hair may be different shades of the same colour, but the texture must be the same. Ear shape, oddly enough, is another characteristic which must be similar in identical twins as it is another genetic marker.

Parents will often quote what the hospital told them at the birth of their twins as proof of the zygocity, but it used to be thought that by rule of thumb identical twins always had one placenta and fraternal twins had two. In the sixties, however, research showed that two placentas fused together could often be mistaken for one at the birth, and that some early divisions of the zygote could, as we have seen, allow each identical twin to develop a placenta of his own. In fact, only one type of placenta can conclusively be shown to belong to mono-zygotic twins. As one can still see where the chorion and amnion were attached to the placenta after the birth any placenta with only one chorion must belong to mono-zygotic twins.

## AFTERBIRTH
## OR PLACENTAL EVIDENCE OF ZYGOCITY
## OF TWINS

### Dizygotic twins          Monozygotic twins

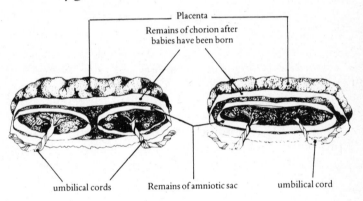

Placenta

Remains of chorion after babies have been born

umbilical cords      Remains of amniotic sac      umbilical cord

Any placenta with only one chorion must belong to monozygotic twins

Unfortunately by the time twins themselves are interested in the subject, placental evidence available at their birth has been destroyed. Other methods like the comparison of the number of lines in the pattern of fingerprints need an expert eye and a knowledge of dermatoglyphics. Recently however, research workers in the field of genetics who also have to be able to classify the twins they compare into the two different groups, made the interesting discovery that very often "mothers know best".

Using questionnaires, they invited the parents of a sample of twins who had previously been classified by blood tests, to say to which type they thought their children belonged. The accuracy of their replies was so interesting that visits were made to the few who had disagreed with the blood test verdicts. In almost every case mothers said that as it had been an official form they had entered what their hospital had told them at the birth but that in their hearts they had never agreed with that diagnosis. Even a few who stuck to their opinions despite the evidence of the blood tests were vindicated when these tests were re-run, and in every case it was found that the laboratory had made an error! It is interesting to know that parents' opinion about their children's zygocity was so reliable. The key question on which it usually hung was, "Have you at any time mistaken one child for the other?" and if the answer is 'yes' then it is 98%–99% sure that that pair are genetically identical.

### Who has twins?

Science has been able to tell us quite a lot about the biology of twins. It can also tell us who has twins and why. No one yet knows just why a zygote splits to form identical twins but what we do know is that it has the same chance of happening to any mother anywhere. A worldwide rate of three pairs of identical twins per thousand maternities seems to be constant whatever the country or culture. The birth rate of fraternal twins, however, has been found to vary according to the mother's age, the number already in her family and the race to which she belongs. Twins or triplets are born to Nigerian mothers about once in every twenty births, but among mothers of the mongoloid races of China, Japan, Vietnam and Korea the rate for twins is only about four per thousand. As three of these twins are likely to be identical we can see that at one in a thousand, fraternal twins are extremely rare in this racial group.

Our own rate of one in a hundred births is roughly equal to that of the Asian Indians, but even within the mixed populations of Europe minor ethnic variations in the national rates can be seen. In France, for example, more twins are born to mothers in Brittany where the people are of Celtic origin. In Britain too we see a slightly higher twinning rate among the Celtic peoples of

Wales, Ireland and the Scots who live in the Western Isles.

Older women stand a higher chance of giving birth to non-identical twins than do their young contemporaries. After the age of thirty-five there is often a surge in the secretion of the hormone which stimulates ovulation. In some families this accounts for the 'second thought' baby born after the rest of the family are well into their teens but for others it results in a double ovulation which leads to the birth of twins.

This natural occurrence can also be induced by drugs so that previously infertile couples have a better chance to conceive. In the 1950s when this technique was first tried it took some time to get the prescription right so that not only was one egg released but seven, eight, and in one case a frightening fifteen (none of whom survived). Now, however, the usual result of this treatment is one baby but there is still the odd occasion when the bonus of two will appear.

Getting it right for couples who long for a family is a delicate matter. For this reason the so-called 'test tube' babies have become another source of twins and even of the higher multiples. In this case, eggs are taken from the mother's ovaries and fertilized by the father's sperm outside her body. Those that are viable are then implanted into the wall of the womb. As implantation itself may be the mother's problem the surgeon will usually implant more than one zygote, in the hope that at least one will take. Should all of them 'take' there will then be a multiple birth.

Although the resulting infants are usually non-identical because each has developed from an individual zygote, one recent case made medical headlines. A set of triplets resulted where only two of the four implanted zygotes had survived. Three babies were born because one of the two remaining zygotes had split and developed into a pair of identical twins.

The physical sciences contribute a lot to our knowledge of the origin and the incidence of twins, but once they have been born we need to turn to social science for some indication of what happens to them next.

# CHAPTER 5

# *Parenting pairs is different*

Setting out as one of a pair is not the safest way to start one's life. In many cases the womb seems to sense very early that something is different and miscarries twin babies. Later, even when a pregnancy has gone well, perhaps responding to the appropriate weight for one baby, the body will go into labour early and twins are born too soon.

Where two healthy babies are carried full term, complications can still arise at the birth. The simple fact that the second twin is held up by the slow progress of the first can cause serious distress, and sometimes the complex circulation problems of those who have shared a placenta become critical for all concerned.

Prematurity in a baby who is a twin however is not quite so serious as it is in the case of a single born infant. It does mean however that over 30% of twins have their first experience of life in the rarefied atmosphere of a special care baby unit.

"My daughter 4lb 4oz did not breathe when born and they said she might be brain damaged. I had to leave her in hospital when I brought her brother home. I was allowed to go to the hospital to feed her—I felt she was a stranger to me as I had not been able to hold her at all when she was born."

Although hospital attitudes have changed drastically over the last few years this mother's experience may well revive memories for other mothers of twins. Not only is their very arrival a struggle but when twins do emerge into the world many of them miss out on that first reassuring contact with their mothers that researchers now feel to be the ideal welcome for the new born child.

Even the birth of the healthiest twin babies can mean a period of emotional adjustment for their parents. The euphoria which usually follows the birth of one new child can be delayed for some time after the birth of twins.

Amazingly it is not easy to tell which mothers are carrying two babies instead of one. Despite modern technology it still happens that a second infant can surprise everyone in the delivery room. Astonishment for the onlookers can be a state of shock for the parents. Guilt at having cried out in labour, "But I only wanted one baby!" or anxiety at having added to the family's already stretched finances can overshadow what should have been a happy event.

Those who know twins are expected find themselves little better prepared. Some mothers who had confidently expected a matching pair later confess to secret disappointment in the days following the birth at finding that their set did not match. Others who had been geared up to make sure they treated their twins as individuals from the start may be distressed to discover that even they cannot tell them apart.

In addition to these particular difficulties parents who have twins are being asked to fall in love with two people at once. It is not unusual for some mothers to suffer secret pangs at this stage on discovering that they seem to have begun to prefer one twin to the other.

Once a family has left hospital however and the babies begin to reveal their individual characteristics most of these emotional problems begin to sort themselves out. Unfortunately they are almost immediately replaced by the common practical frustrations of trying to care for two infants at once.

"Mine were both premature. They needed three-hourly feeding but they were so slow that each feed took two hours, leaving me an hour in which to do everything else!"

One can only hope that the expectant father who expressed bewilderment as to why one baby should take up so much time in the day did not find that his wife had presented him with twins. Another mother remembers,

"I had no pregnancy problems and both boys were very healthy babies, both almost 6lb in weight. We found a super home help who came in at least twice a week and support of friends was marvellous. Even with all this, my day began at 6.00 am and ended at 11.00 pm. No middle of the night feeds, for I had to get some sleep. Even so, I was constantly tired for the first two and a half years."

Practical problems are often added to what has already been a difficult day. The twin pram will not go through the supermarket checkout. Getting on a bus with two babies and a folding pushchair is almost impossible. The back seat of even a Rolls Royce will not accommodate two carrycots to allow parents to make even the simplest journey to the clinic with their babies. On top of all this, the smiling comment of the passerby who says, "Twins, how nice!" serves only to underline the gulf which lies between society's fond expectations and the harsh realities of life for the parents concerned.

The arrival of twins in a family can induce an atmosphere of stress. American research has identified infant twins in a high proportion of families reported for "baby battering" or child abuse. There is no evidence in this country that twin children are any more at risk of abuse than any others but having had their own days of mounting despair many twin parents will understand how such things might well occur.

"Particularly when they were babies when they woke at the same time crying for their three-hourly feeds, my stomach used to turn over. I'd wonder how I would feed one when the other baby was howling. While I fed the first baby I'd leave the other in his pram in another room and switch the radio on loudly so I could not hear the other one crying and carry on feeding the first one."

Anyone who has seen a mother pick up two toddlers and struggle to open a door with her nonexistent third hand will agree that from a practical point of view parenting pairs is different.

In Britain up and down the country small groups of parents of twins found that meeting and sharing their frustrations gave them much needed support. In 1979 twelve groups met together to found what is now called the Twins and Multiple Births Association (TAMBA). Their main aim was to provide an umbrella address where mothers nationwide could write to discover whether there might be a local group for them. Thanks to the crusading zeal of Judy Linney, the first president, her reply "No, there is no club near you but why don't you set one up?" resulted in the foundation of 200 new clubs within the first two years.

What this illustrates is the widespread need in parents of twins for public acknowledgment that their situation is indeed somewhat different. This is in fact a universal need among parents who have had a multiple birth. TAMBA soon discovered sister organisations already in existence worldwide. America has a stateswide Mother of Twins Club. Canada has a lively Parents of Multiple Births Association. In Europe, the Netherlands also has support groups. South Africa has two and Australia has an extremely active Multiple Births Organisation which successfully lobbied parliament to improve the grant support for mothers of triplets. Japan too, despite having one of the lowest twinning rates, long ago recognised the special status of the mother of twins and boasts one of the oldest of these associations. The mutual support given locally to ordinary mothers by others in their neightbourhood is augmented by the work of the main associations, who deal with special needs as they arise. Leaflets are available on coping with premature twins, toilet training two at once, and with sleepless nights. Support groups also exist for those mourning the loss of one or both twins, and at the other end of the scale for those coping with triplets or more. One glance at the scope of their work is enough to show the problems presented to parents of multiple births as being on a different scale from those encountered when babies arrive one at a time. Practical help is a must but there are many underlying stresses and strains which surprise us and which can only be resolved by the parents themselves. Research is beginning to suggest that parenting pairs would still be different even if there were ninety nannies to do the extra work and to prevent the practical problems.

During 1980, three quite separate psychologists published findings about parents and their twins. In Israel a team discovered that while mothers of twins spent an average of 35–37% of their time with their babies, mothers of single infants, who very often had other children as well, spent an average of 22–29% of their time with them. "Lucky for her that she was able to," might be one's response to this piece of information. Mothers of twins often regret not having had time to enjoy their baby days. One mother remembers,

"It was such a shame I never had time to enjoy them. If only they had been born with a gap between them they would not have had to share me at such a crucial age."

But what the researchers believed they were observing was not merely the inability of busy mothers to give time to their babies but an actual subconscious withdrawal from spending time with them.

When the research was widened to look at parents of triplets and quads the observers were at first puzzled to discover that these mothers spent even less time with their babies despite the generous help of resident nurses and a home help service provided by the government. Parents of these babies not only spent time away from their babies but actually out of the house, as if taking the opportunity to escape from a situation that overwhelmed them.

Mothers of twins are of course faced with quite different problems from those of mothers of triplets or quads, but as it is normal for human mothers to relate to one baby at a time, the effect of increasing this number by even one seems to trigger a wish to withdraw. On a less deep level, one can see for example that the incentive for a mother to go and pick up one baby alone on his own is likely to be stronger than for the mother to approach twins apparently content in each other's company.

However we phrase it, it looks as though infant twins are likely to have less contact with their mothers than single babies. This could be significant as the quality of an infant's contact with a caring adult is known to shape his social and emotional development as a child.

Mothers with new babies spend long periods studying their faces. One mother described this as "Drinking him in" or as a ritual "Getting to know you". Researchers now feel that this eye to eye contact is not just a sentimental exercise but an important phase in the process of establishing attachment between the mother and child. Mothers of twins however can find this process of bonding complicated by the need to be fair. Trying not to spend too long with one baby she may tend to alternate this eye contact so instead of 'having a long drink' she gets to know her babies by a 'series of sips'.

A second piece of research done in South Africa has shown that this pattern of contact between mothers and their twins persists beyond infancy. In a study of how we learn to speak, films were made of mothers playing with their toddlers. The mothers with one baby focused directly on them, talking to them, showing them toys and laughing with them. Where the toddlers were twins however, instead of the steady eye contact mothers had exchanged with one child, mothers of twins divided their attention rapidly between their two children so that neither benefited from prolonged contact. When the films of twin mothers were slowed down and examined frame by frame, an average of twenty-six shifts of visual attention were counted in the first three minutes that they ran. When a mother tried to attend to two children at once the record read, "Mother looks at twin two while her hand is still stretched out to twin one."

Obviously there will be times when this happens in other families where pre-school children are close in age. For twins however this is not an occasional but a normal pattern of contact with their mother. Not only is one's twin there all the time but he always requires exactly the same quality of attention from his mother at exactly the same time.

With spaced children, a cuddle and a tickle will usually reassure a toddler that his mother is aware of his presence and his need for her. The fact that she is at the same time pointing out a picture to his baby sister will not detract from the quality of her contact with him. It may even enhance it, being a secret between them, of which the baby is not aware.

With pre-school twins this will almost never happen. All parents of twin toddlers are familiar with urgent demands of "Do it to me! Do it to me!" when Miss Eagle Eye spots a smile or a gesture that has been directed towards her sister and not to her. Some parents report that a twin of this age will even demand the repetition of a whole sentence, word for word. It is not that they have not heard what was said but that they demand the same attention they feel their twin has had.

Twins in this situation may not only be demanding more attention. They may also quite simply be trying to stimulate more speech from their parents. The third piece of research which came from Canada revealed that on an actual count of words and gestures parents of twins talked less to their children than did matched parents with two toddlers of roughly the same age. The only significant difference between the parents of two-year-old twins and those with two sons eighteen and twenty-eight months old, was the fact that the twins were being seen as a pair. This once again seemed to confirm that a subconscious force is at work on adults which elicits a different response when they are parenting pairs.

Research projects done under laboratory conditions sometimes seem rather removed from our own experience in real life. Sometimes however we can call up incidents from our own experience which do in fact echo what they have to say.

There is a lot of enjoyment to be had from just watching twin toddlers. One family wrote:

"We have an amusing film of the twins about fifteen months, just toddling — where the girl literally made all the first moves — walking down the paths between the rose bushes. Everything she did the boy copied and he followed in her wake absolutely."

The adults here were entranced by what was almost a performance: they did not want to interrupt. In fact everybody probably sat with bated breath for fear of distracting the children before father returned with the camera.

In the same group, a single child might also have been the star of the show but he would have been cheered on and verbally encouraged.

"What a clever boy!", "Oops a Daisy", "There, try it again". Everyone would urge him to continue to amuse them.

In our contact with twin children however we are often inhibited from using natural *verbal* encouragement because they are acting like a pair. Their 'performance' is seen to be as much for each other as for us. Play between twins at this age will sometimes take the form of a wordless mosaic of action and reaction which looks so like some sophisticated form of communication that one hesitates to cut across it with anything as crude as human speech.

### The pair effect

It is difficult to resist this pressure to perceive pre-school twins as a pair. Despite the apparently obvious difference of boy and girl, dark and fair, the fact that they are zipped into similar playsuits, strapped into the same stroller, and then pushed to the same playground, loads the dice against the efforts we may make to keep them apart in our minds.

Once behaviour and speech develop, and as each child's individual personality has emerged, parents may find it difficult to believe that they once reacted to their children as a unit of two. According to research however, these early days when adults are most susceptible to this "Pair effect", are the most crucial for the foundation of our children's future social skills, and as we will see there are areas where this "paired" element of early experience does tend to leave a mark.

# CHAPTER 6

# The bright side of the coin

The last chapter may have made depressing reading as it began to sound like the build up to some statement of the inferiority of twins. Phrases like 'traumatic birth into an atmosphere of family tensions', 'less than normal contact with mother' and 'less experience of speech' occur in discussions about childhood deprivation and behaviour problems in later life. On the contrary, however, children who are twins have been found to be a remarkably stable group.

Children who cause their parents and teachers concern are referred for expert help to Child Guidance Clinics which form a part of the school psychological service. Any twins showing symptoms of behaviour difficulties would have found their way there. In order to fill out the picture for this book, clinics in various parts of the country were approached and asked to check how many twin children they had seen during three previous years.

Two clinics were sufficiently intrigued by the question to extend their search of past files up to ten years but in neither case could they find any trace of any child who had been a twin. Another clinic, covering an area of very high incidence of twin births, had seen only one, and of the others who sent numbers three was the highest given.

Of the small group of twins who had been seen, only a tiny percentage had been referred because of behaviour problems. Most had been sent for re-testing by the psychologist because their class performance did not come up to what their measured IQ would have led their teachers to expect.

In America a similar enquiry found that twin children were referred for Child Guidance less often than might have been expected in relation to their known incidence in the population. The implication of this finding is that the special circumstances of twins' early life, which have been found to affect the emotional stability of single children, do not appear to affect them. Being seen as a pair initially may have disadvantages, but in the event, this very two-ness of twins somehow manages also to invoke sufficient positive behaviour to ensure that they do not miss out.

## A Special Role for Fathers

Where some first-time fathers may be rather uncertain of their role as mother and baby seem to form an exclusive unit, a father of twins will usually have his role as joint caretaker confirmed for him right at the start. Research shows that infant twins are far more likely to be fed and changed by their fathers. In the Canadian study we referred to earlier, it was noticed that the twin toddlers were more likely to approach their father, even if their mother was present, than were the single spaced children who tended to choose their mother even where they had to wait their turn. A 'father effect' was found to be at work acting positively for twins even in his absence. Mothers of single parent families who had twins talked more to their children than did both parents put together in other twin families. These mothers did the work of two in actively trying to make up to their babies for the lack of a father.

The original theory that the mother/child relationship is the one which is central to healthy human emotional development, has more recently been modified to include a child's early relationship with any consistent adults in his environment who share his mother's role. The emotional stability of children who are twins could therefore owe a lot to this early involvement of both parents in their daily care. A baby who can relate to both father and mother is more likely to be emotionally secure at the approach of strangers, for example, than one for whom their mother alone represents their anchor in life.

## Twins and their twin

The theories which deal exclusively with mother/infant relation-ship not only ignore the part played by fathers but that which is played by an infant's siblings too. In general this is probably quite correct. Siblings may not normally have much contact with a new baby who spends most of his time asleep. An infant twin however spends more time in the company of his twin than he does with his mother. What is more, this is how it has been from before he was born.

Mothers can feel the movements of their babies in the womb. It is possible that twin babies are aware of each other's movements too. Awareness of 'an other' is their normal experience before birth, and after birth the physical awareness of that other presence can reassure an infant twin. Several mothers have found that to settle a restless infant in the same cot as his twin will work wonders where hours of rocking in their arms has failed to calm him down.

The idea that twins may be aware of each other in the womb may be supported by the strange awareness of twinship which seems to haunt some single survivors of a twin birth.

"I was one of twins. My brother died at birth, my mother was too ill even to be shown the baby and all the doctor did was to emphasise how 'bonny' I was and how 'lucky' she was to have me. They chose not to tell me about my twin and as I was a very large baby she half believed that her expectation of twins must have been a false alarm. No one seems to have thought about me. As I grew into a toddler I was seen to run to my own mirror reflection and often chattered baby talk to it excitedly—and more disturbing, as I walked along the road with her my mother noted how often I looked back and waited as though for someone else. In the end she went to the doctor, who, because of my 'symptoms', told her at last that I was in fact one of twins. The doctor was as surprised as my parents that somehow, young as I was, I seemed to 'know' that I should not be alone . . . even now when I am a mother of two children of my own . . . I realise that the subconscious part of me is still searching for my twin."

It is easy to be sceptical of stories like this but it is the frequency rather than the content of such claims which makes one wonder. It is also worth noting that those who claim to have this conviction that they were part of a pair are not necessarily happy to have the sensation. Re-united twins who had grown up not knowing of their twinship express relief that this persistent feeling has in the end proved to be founded on fact and not, as they had sometimes feared, to be a symptom of some kind of delusion.

Even if infant twins are not aware of each other in the womb, once they are born close physical contact is their everyday experience. Most twins share a pram. At first they may sleep in the same cot, and photographs of sleeping twins each sucking the other's thumbs are not uncommon.

As we have seen, for a variety of reasons mothers of twins tend to pick them up less frequently than they would have had they been on their own.

"If one was crying and I lifted him, the other would start too, so I tried to comfort him still in his cot without picking him up," said one mother, and another remembered,

"I just found that two slings, one back and one on the front, got far too heavy early on."

To some infant twins, falling asleep in the warmth of each other's body offers a similar reassurance to falling asleep in their mother's arms. Even when the going is rough, twins together can give each other the comfort of consistent physical contact without which a single baby in the same situation might feel abandoned and alone.

'Getting to know you' works here too. It used to be thought that twins sucking each other's thumbs were bound to grow up with a confused idea of where their own body ended and where their twin's began, but it has been pointed out that a sharp bite or kick will very quickly define which bits belong to whom. 'Getting to know you' through physical contact is actually an effective way of 'getting to know me' too. Far from being confused, infant twins are probably more aware of their own physical outline much earlier than single children at the same stage. Alone in his pram, one baby has to postpone his exploration of himself in relation to others until an adult appears who has time to pick him up.

## More contact — not less

Lying close together will allow infant twins to become aware of each other visually at a very early date. The focusing distance of infants' eyes is quite short but the distance between twins in a side by side pram is just about right. Quite early on, twin babies can be seen to study each other's faces and long before they can talk they seem to exchange glances that are meaningful. Eye contact becomes a form of communication between twin children just as it will later on between each individual twin and his mother. Because twin babies have the opportunity to practise this for long periods between themselves, this form of communication, for some pairs, will acquire a very special significance.

In the past, twins have been known to develop their own private language. In extreme cases this has involved strange words and even a complicated grammatical structure. Most adult twins who remember such secret communication however refer to a language of eye contact rather than one which used words. Some twins even give clear examples of its use.

"At school we used eye language. I used to flick the answer to her if she did not know it," said one girl.

In almost every area where research seems to indicate a pair effect at work between twins and their parents, twinship itself seems to offer some compensation. Even sensitivity to a tense family atmosphere can be cushioned by the presence of one's twin in childhood as many adult twins can recall.

"Despite or maybe because we were unhappy I have warm feelings going back to my childhood that my sister was something of 'My own', and I still feel like that now."

Some years ago, a Russian psychologist was able to gain some idea of the extent to which twin children can draw on each other for the support and encouragement normally supplied by a parent. In 1976 Madame Kuluchova was called in to help rehabilitate seven-year-old twin boys who had been kept in a cellar by their stepmother for six years, and cruelly treated. Sadly, this was not the first case of its kind. There have been several studies of children who have been locked away from human contact, and of 'wild' children found abandoned in woods and forests. Few emerge as unscathed as Rudyard Kipling's Mowgli of the *Jungle Book*. Almost all function at a sub-normal level. They have no speech and seem incapable of learning any language even in happier times.

Kuluchova's twins however, despite being found in such an extreme stage of physical neglect that neither of them could stand, had not suffered from this sort of intellectual set-back. Once recovered and settled happily in a foster home they made great progress and to everyone's surprise they were eventually able to attend school and to compete on a level with their contemporaries.

One can well imagine that these little boys were able to comfort each other phsyically, but the fact that they were able to offer each other sufficient mental stimulation to prevent permanent damage to their learning ability was seen by Madame Kuluchova as a direct result of their twinship.

During the first years of life, the subconscious development of support between twins establishes a stable foundation on which the emotional and social structure of their personalities will later be built. This mutual development does not however mean that they will go on to form a closed unit needing nobody else. Given a choice, a twin toddler will always choose his mother's company rather than that of his twin. Infant twins, as they grow, build up two bonds of attachment; the one with their mother and the other with their twin, and in some cases if they are allowed to, both relationships will develop along very similar lines, but in the case of the sibling bond the "pair effect" may interfere. Between a mother and her child consistent caring will forge a bond which is then paradoxically strong enough for the child to leave the mother happily when the time has come. Staying home with grandma while she goes to the shops proves to the toddler that the tie between him and his mother can survive her absence. By the age of three or four, most children's trust in their mothers' continued concern for them is no longer dependent on her tangible presence in their vicinity.

Attachment for twins can follow the same path. Separate visits to grandma at this stage would strengthen their bond in the same way. The pair effect however, together with practical considerations, will often mean that very young twins are never exposed to dealing with separation and go everywhere together. For some of them the support of their twin may be allowed to become synonymous with his actual physical presence, and at a much later date when they have the chance to test the invisible strength of the bond between them panic may prevent their proving its worth.

For the time being, however, setting out together most twin children will meet the world as well equipped as any singleton for a happy and well-adjusted childhood. The early differences in their experience seem to even out and the behaviour of those pairs who spend vast amounts of their time scrapping with each other can be put down to normal nuisance rather than to the unhappy attention seeking behaviour of deprived children who have missed out through having been born as twins.

Twin children approach their school days at no greater disadvantage in their emotional and personality development than other single born brothers and sisters. They may even be emotionally more stable and personally more secure because of their partnership. There are, however, some specific areas where only their twinship can account for differences which have been found between them and their single born peers.

For years, researchers puzzled over test results where twins as a group presented a contrast to their single born friends of the same age. It became customary to put this down in blanket terms as due to something in 'the twin situation'. But as these differences related to some of the areas which are highest on most parents' lists of things that cause concern it might be best to give them a chapter of their own.

Having been reassured in this chapter that twins are likely to be personally more stable and emotionally more secure than their singleton peers, it may come as a shock to learn that as a group in the past they have been regarded by psychologists as slower to speak, retarded as readers, and generally to gain lower scores in tests of intelligence.

# CHAPTER 7

# *But twins are slower, aren't they?*

As long ago as the 1920s, psychologists began to notice that when they tested the intelligence of a very large sample of children, the average score for the group who were twins among them was always lower than the average for the singleton group. This does not mean, however, that all twins are dim.

Any group whose average IQ is low may still have within it people who are extremely bright. Average scores are not about individuals. They indicate, where they vary from the norm, the existence of some common factor which is affecting the majority performance. If this factor can be found one may be able to correct it and so improve the performance of the group as a whole.

In the case of twins, forty years were to pass before there was any hint of what their common factor might be. It was in fact quite surprising that its presence was picked up at all as the size of the difference in question was only a matter of five or six points. The average for singleton children would work out at 100 on the IQ scale while the average for the group who were twins would consistently come out at around 95.

If these numbers are to mean anything at all we need to know what they imply. As a rule of thumb children of average ability in a normal school will score between 105–96 on the IQ scale. Those who have to work to keep up score between 95–86, and those struggling but still capable, between 84–71. The question of remedial teaching will only arise if children are scoring between 74–50 points. In these studies therefore twins were not being labelled as retarded but merely as having a tendency to come towards the middle to lower end of a normal school group.

It was nevertheless worth searching for the cause to see if the deficit might not be reversed. As it was known that more than half of all twins born weigh less than five pounds at birth, one theory was that it might be a hangover from their poor start in life. Others wondered whether as intelligence tended to correlate with social class it was merely a matter of more twins having been born into the lower socio-economic groups and so pulling the average down.

When this last suggestion was tested however it became clear that whatever was causing the problem affected twins in all the socio-economic groups. On the graph, as expected, the scores for the singleton groups dipped as one went down the post-master general's scale of social class but although the graphs for the twin groups followed the same path exactly they did so at a fixed amount lower in every case.

Graph showing how twin group IQ's lag behind singleton IQ's by the same amount, no matter which socio-economic class

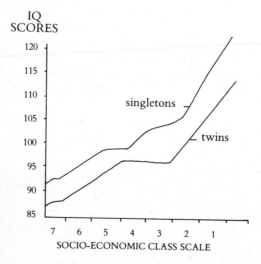

from Zazzo 1960 in *Les Jeaumeaux: Le Couple et La Personne*

This meant that the intelligence of twin children was depressed by the same sort of things that depressed the intelligence of single children, but it still did not explain why in each class group the twins' scores were lower still. There was still no answer in 1953 when the Scottish Council for Research in Education found this discrepancy once again. After 70,000 children were tested, 947 of whom were twins, their report concluded rather lamely:

" . . . the intellectual inferiority of twins . . . is probably due to factors inherent in twinning as such."

By the mid-sixties, however, there was a glimmer of light. An American psychologist, Helen Koch, carrying out a study of forty pairs of six-year-old twins, used a different type of test to measure their intelligence. This was the Thurston Primary Abilities test which gives separate consideration to five different aspects of ability: verbal, perceptual, quantitative, motor and spacial. Helen Koch's twins did better than single children in spacial tests, matched them in most others, but their results in the tests of verbal reasoning were quite significantly bad.

Back in Britain, a verbal reasoning test had been included for some time in the '11+ examination' which was then taken by every child before he or she left primary school. Researchers were therefore able to look at these results, and sure enough, the average for singleton children was 100.1 and that for twins 95.7. It so happened however that this sample included 148 children who had been born as twins but who having lost their twin at birth had grown up as single born children.

If the average score of this group were to turn out similar to that of the twin pairs it would confirm that the twin deficit was irreversible and due to lingering effects of their having shared their pregnancies and births. If it turned out to be nearer to that of the single children then it must be due to something which had happened after they had been born, in which case something could be done about it.

The result of this important study was that the average score for surviving twins was 98.8, sufficiently nearer to that of the singleton group to prove that twins do come into the world with the same sort of intelligence potential as any other children, and that whatever it is that happens to them does so as they grow up.

The connection between verbal ability and measurable intelligence in twins was then illustrated quite dramatically in one specific case. A pair of identical girls were referred to the American psychologist, Gesell, when they started school with very poor speech. They were given intensive speech therapy over a period of months, although their identical IQ of 69 meant they were unlikely to improve. After eight months the girls were re-tested and although a slight improvement was expected, one twin's jump from 69 to 105 amazed the teachers. Her sister's rise from 69 to 89, though not quite so dramatic, was also an unexpected surprise. These tests, which had not been made on speech alone, showed that there had been an all-round improvement as a result of the improvement in their speech.

Verbal reasoning ability, which is what psychologists call the way we use and understand our language, relates back to the way in which we first learn to speak. As a result of these studies health visitors and those closely involved with the development of young children began to warn parents to be alert if their twins were slow to speak. If this was the case then speech therapy was recommended and initial problems were almost always overcome.

It had been assumed by everyone that once twins had grasped the essentials of articulation all would be well, but the real message of the IQ studies had been missed. Some twins do develop severe speech difficulties but not every twin has this problem. The IQ studies had in fact pointed to a more general twin handicap in verbal reasoning which could result from *the way* that the majority had learned to communicate. As we have seen in the last chapter, recent research is now showing that this is one area where experience is different for children who are twins.

Every child comes to a critical stage of development at which he is ready for the next step forward. If his circumstances do not provide the stimulation which he needs to move on to the next stage he will often take something that approximates to it and arrive at the same goal by a less efficient route. Babies who teach themselves to 'bottom shuffle' rather than to crawl take much longer actually to walk. They are already in the 'head up' position so do not need to pull themselves up to see what is going on, their weight bearing muscles do not get as much exercise as those of the babies who crawl and their incentive to get up and walk becomes very much less.

*Learning to speak has a parallel*

On average, human babies are ready to learn to communicate somewhere between eighteen months and three years. Long before this, however, twins have picked up the essential technique of exchanging signs which is the basis of language. All they need now is someone to tell them which sound they should use. Twins who do not have sufficient opportunity or special encouragement to speak with adults will continue to develop the form of communication they have discovered between themselves. Like the bottom shuffling baby, they will get there in the end, and learn their mother's tongue too, but having started along their own way of communication these twins will have to retrace their steps and re-code their already filed understanding of 'meaning' into speech.

What we file in our memory is 'meaning' rather than the actual spoken word, as I discovered during a French examination one day. In translation I needed to use a French word which I remembered shouting at one of the children I had played with during my time in France. I remembered the scene and what I had said to her in French, but it was the meaning I had registered and the word itself I could not recall.

Some evidence from Australia now ties up initial problems of speech with later difficulties in learning to read. Reading has been found to be a common problem among twin boys, many of whom have problems with fluency and are what is termed slow readers. Those who have had early problems with speech however have other difficulties as well, making mistakes which are more easily associated with accuracy and 'coding', which relates to this tie up of meaning with what appears on the printed page.

*What can we do then?*

Twins who do have sufficient opportunity for speech with the adults around them actually achieve speech earlier and not later than other children. Those talkative parents who bore their neighbours are a boon to their babies. Twins, given lots of exposure to the spoken word, will by-pass baby talk and start by speaking in sentences. One mother remembers how this happened in her family.

"During their first two years they never talked but would look at each other, nod, and go and do something. Communicating with other children was through mime. It seemed as though they couldn't understand why other people didn't read their thoughts as they did. They had no spoken twin language and once they did begin to speak properly they spoke in sentences and have never shut up since."

Given the necessary exposure to vocabulary twins quickly cotton on. Another mother told how her twins taught each other to speak.

"They seemed to learn any new vocabulary on the same day and practise it with each other in their cots at night."

But if what they are practising is inaccurate they will learn it just the same.

Twins do then differ from other brothers and sisters in that they have a potential advantage where communication is concerned and the key to making sure that they follow it up is to offer them constant conversation from the start. Unfortunately this potential is too often turned to disadvantage because of society's insistence on regarding twins as a pair. Most pram designers, for example, dictate that twins should face each other and not the adult they are with. If it rains, hoods hide them right away, and later on as toddlers in twin buggies they neither face each other nor their mother as the handles are placed for her to push from behind.

Time spent in a pram of the right type can be precious for twins as it provides that exclusive face to face encounter with their mother which they have so seldom at home. Singing, laughing, talking, and pointing out things of interest are all lost on children of this age unless they can see the visual clues of gesture and expression which accompany the words. The connection between speech and the development of intelligence is so important that even the choice of prams and pushchairs should be viewed with this in mind.

At home there are other things which militate against twins hearing enough adult speech. Just when they would benefit most from conversation they will themselves sometimes create an inhibiting atmosphere.

"They did not have a language of words, more looks, that seemed to be a form of communication which constantly made me feel left out," said one mother.

This was sufficient to diminish her first intention of talking to them. Feeling that they did not want her she would change her mind, return to the kitchen and do her washing up instead.

It has been proved, however, that despite this impression of exclusiveness twins will always choose speech with an adult, if offered, to conversation with their twin.

"Before my boy and girl talked," one mother said, "they had a language of their own. It was as though they just enjoyed speaking to each other without anyone knowing what they meant."

When they appear to exclude others it is often an expression of their enjoyment of this complicity rather than a proof of their wish to be left alone.

Once having opened a conversation with baby twins, however, the problem of repetition can make it hard going for the adult. With one baby one shapes the letters in an exaggerated way so he can see how they are formed.

"Bubbles, Yes Bubb—les!"

Talking like this to two children is not only awkward but tiring too. After a while one will in fact stop repeating and talk only to the most interested twin. Once twins are old enough to respond in conversation, research also shows that adults almost invariably talk most to the one who already speaks best.

In most situations pre-school twins are in competition for the adult they are with. Having once gained his attention the twin who is most advanced in speech will hold on to his advantage. Parents will be familiar with this no-pause-for-breath conversation of the youngster who is determined to prevent any interruption from his twin. If this continues to happen the quieter twin may just give up and his speech become so hesitant that even adults will try to hurry him when he does have something to say.

It is not difficult to see how some of these pair-induced situations can be avoided but our very language that we teach our twins also has pitfalls of which we need to be aware. For some twins, singulars and plurals take a life-time to unravel. My letters from twins frequently begin:

"I are a twin," "I am one of a twin" or "I am half of a twin." The rest of the letter follows with perfect grammar until the next singular/plural hazard raises its head.

"It would be nice for her just to be there if I wanted to tell us something," wrote one girl and "When we were independent of ourselves," said another.

As English no longer uses the singular pronoun 'thou', sentences which contain 'You' must always be ambiguous when addressed to twins.

The question—"Did you have a nice time in the park?" may either be answered by both children, by the same child every time, or by neither one, as each waits for the other to respond. Parents who do not make a point of calling their twins by name from birth will find that at seven or eight years old twins will completely ignore their requests if they are phrased as—

"Will you please shut the door," or "Pick that up before someone falls over it."

The exasperation felt by the ignored adult usually masks this genuine confusion which needs to be sorted out. The behaviour of one member of a family is rarely the 'property' of that one alone. Pair responses may initially be made by the parents but if we are not careful they will in the end also be used by the twins themselves.

Nowadays, twins are less likely to be treated as a pair because the adults who are close to them are more aware of the need to respond consciously to each child. Already wider knowledge of research into speech and intelligence has meant fewer instances of twin language are being found among twins starting school. Replies to my own questionnaire covering 600 twins and their parents mentioned only seventeen cases, fourteen of which had disappeared by the time the twins were five years of age.

A change in attitude can therefore decrease the effects of being brought up as a pair but questions still remain as to other areas where twins may affect each other within their pair.

# CHAPTER 8

# How twinship works

One of Charles Darwin's cousins, Sir Francis Galton, was the first scientist to use twins in his studies. He thought, quite rightly, that identical twins must share the same genetic origin, or as he put it, the same 'Nature'. If they were brought up together then they would share the same 'Nurture' too. Fraternal twins, on the other hand, would have only their Nurture in common. If this were so, he surmised, then a comparison of the two types should help him discover which areas of development were hereditary and which were due to the influence of the environment in which they had been brought up.

Twin studies are still being done today. If more identical twins share a trait than do fraternal twins then it is generally assumed to result from their common heredity rather than from their common environment. In one study it was found, for example, that if one member of an identical set suffered from motion sickness then so would his twin. Although many individual fraternal twins were affected, both twins become ill in only 27% of these pairs. Motion sickness is an easily identifiable state which can be studied under laboratory conditions so it would seem reasonable to assume that what had been found to be hereditary among twins would be hereditary among non-twins.

Twin studies however have not been confined to the more precise areas of physiological research. They have also been used in the less well-defined areas of psychological and sociological study. Unfortunately, whereas in the field of pathology the discovery of a negative trait might lead to its elimination by genetic counselling, in these less specific areas the discovery of a positive genetic trait which can be passed on can carry with it overtones which are rather sinister.

If, for example, it could be proved that only intelligent people have intelligent children, a government might make it their policy to encourage only those above a certain IQ to have children. If because of this hereditary connection it was also believed that no amount of education could alter a given level of intelligence by environmental means, then this government could justify concentrating all its resources solely on the education of those already known to be bright.

In the past, right wing policies have been based on just such assumptions in the hope of producing a master race. For this reason twin studies fell into disfavour for a time and in the USSR, until very recently, they were banned altogether.

Rene Zazzo, a psychologist working in Paris, also questioned the use of twin studies. But his reasons were based on quite different objections. For many years Zazzo had used the comparison of twins in his own work but as he came to know his subjects better he began to doubt whether the results of his twin studies were really directly equivalent to the results he might have got had he been using a similar group of paired singleton individuals drawn from the wider population.

As we have seen ourselves in earlier chapters, there are some areas where twinship adds an extra dimension to the life experience of twins which is not applicable to those who are single born. Zazzo was concerned that there might be yet more undiscovered differences common to twins which as they did not apply to the wider public could invalidate the application of the findings of twin studies to non-twins. Zazzo felt strongly that the experience of twins who had grown up together was affected by what he called a 'couple effect'. Zazzo's 'couple effect' is a much more dynamic description of what had been previously referred to as 'the twin situation'. If we think of railway wagons 'coupled' together we can see that the movement of one will be dictated by the movement of the other—no matter from which end the engine may be pushing or pulling. This concept of 'couple effect' introduces the idea of a continuous process of action and reaction between twins; whatever might be done by one is controlled to some extent by the effect it might have on his partner.

Kay Cassil, the American author of *Twins—Nature's amazing mystery* describes this effect at work in her own experience with her identical twin.

"We look back at a thinly veiled and continuing struggle for dominance, which was always balanced by concern for the other twin's feelings."

The emotional tie here modified the amount of aggression each sister allowed herself to show towards the other, whereas the same sibling rivalry between spaced children would usually take the form of occasional blatant sessions of good healthy hate.

Other mutual constraints within twinships will be less equally balanced than those in this example. Where one child is prettier, more outgoing, or academically more successful, it is not only the less fortunate child who is affected by the comparison. The more favoured twin may suffer guilt that her very existence so constantly highlights this area where her twin fails.

Growing up as a pair, twins will meet many situations like this and one twin, or both, can make a conscious adjustment so that the equilibrium between them is not too drastically disturbed. A clever twin may hold back in class so that comparison between their work will cause less comment, or a slower twin may make it clear to her sister that she enjoys the reflected glory and so ease her concern.

There are however other unconscious adjustments that research has found to be at work between siblings near in age which affect twins too. As these studies were done on pairs of brothers and sisters almost certainly they fit very closely to the five different pairings into which twins fall: identical girls, identical boys, fraternal girls, fraternal boys, and the boy/girl sets.

Helen Koch, the psychologist, who helped to pinpoint verbal reasoning as a problem for twins, studied the intelletual development of singleton children too. One of the intriguing things that she noticed was that the girls who did well in her tests were often those who had a sister near to them in age. On the other hand, the boys who had a brother near in age tended to turn up in the group who had fared worst.

Sutton Smith and Rosenberg, in their book *The Sibling* tell how they followed up this observation with older children. They looked at the results of a college entrance examination. Among the candidates 600 girls and 300 boys were found who came from families of two children born not more than two years apart.

Not only were they able to repeat Helen Koch's results, but also the reverse. The nearer sisters came in age to each other, the better they did academically. The boys who did best, on the other hand, were among those with the widest age gap, and the closer the gap, the less well they seemed to do.

If twins are similar to brothers and sisters we would expect to find that in any group of twins tested together, a spread of girls towards the top of the scale and a preponderance of boys towards the bottom. Because this is only a trend of course, there will also be some bright boys among the better performers and some slower girls among those with lower scores. Sure enough, the poor performance of boy twins as a group, compared with twin girls, has been of particular interest to researchers for some considerable time.

All boys in general, whether twins or not, tend to lag behind girls when tested in the early stages of school work. It is a well known by-word among psychologists that no matter what one may choose to study, the poor old boys will always be found to come out worst; to be at the bottom of the scale; or, if it is a disease, to suffer from it more!

The National Child Development Survey carried out a long-term study of 11,000 children born in 1958. Their report on this sample at seven years of age gave a beautiful picture. It seemed as though classrooms up and down the country were filled with little girls bent busily over their books, while most of the little boys were happily absorbed in what was happening outside the windows. Girls were ahead in reading, in oral work, and they were more creative. Boys, on the other hand, although they lagged behind in the basic subjects, had a better understanding of the world around them. The report described boys as more 'thing orientated' and girls as more 'person orientated'.

There is no need for parents of sons to despair however, as by the mid-teens boys have begun to catch up with their girl classmates and in many cases they will overtake them. Despite this tendency however, an Australian study of literacy and numeracy found boy twins still trailing at the beginning of their teens. Both boy twins and girl twins were found to be competent in number work. Girl twins who had had early reading problems had caught up, but where 70% of single boys had achieved adequate standards of literacy only 42% of boy twins were competent in this regard. Boy twins were therefore seen not to be lagging merely because they were boys or merely because they were twins, but very clearly because they were boys who were twins.

It is now recognised that there is a specific difference between the initial learning pattern of the male and female brain but the ability to learn is not only affected by the biological techniques of information gathering. It is also influenced by environmental factors like physical comfort of the body and emotional comfort of the soul. A student studying for an exam is not likely to absorb much if he is suffering from toothache. His concentration is going to be equally disturbed by the recurring thoughts of his girlfriend, who has just thrown him over. These are extreme examples but they show how other less urgent pressures may also be at work affecting one's capacity to learn.

The National Child Development Survey's comment about girls being more "person orientated" is significant here. It can be matched up with some of the male/female characteristics set out in personality inventory scales. These scales, which rate things like 'aggression' as a masculine trait and those like 'compliance' as a feminine trait, rate a "preference for close social interaction" as a strongly feminine characteristic. If girls are more comfortable than boys in situations of close social contact, then twin girls operate in the atmosphere most closely attuned to their temperament. This also helps to explain why sisters near in age should do so well in school. Boy twins forced into proximity by their double birth may, on the other hand, be forced to operate in a situation foreign to their natural bent.

Among identical twin girls in particular, it is common to find pairs who are academically bright and who seem to maintain their place at the top of the class by a strategy of spurring each other on. Boy twins, and in particular non-identical boy twins, tend to drift near the lower end of the class and in some cases have been described as engaging in negative competition, apparently vying with each other to see who can do worst.

While researching the background for this book, I was fortunate enough to meet the deputy head of a fairly new junior school. Having worked there continuously from the day it had opened, she not only had access to the registers for the past twenty years, but could call to mind the face of each child who had passed through her hands. Fourteen sets of twins had been through this school. Out of the nine male pairs, all six of the non-identical boy pairs had been seen by the child psychologist for failure to perform as well as their measured IQ would have led their teachers to expect.

If we pursue the idea of male and female traits we see that young males in the animal world learn very early to mark out and guard territory for themselves to the exclusion of other males. It may not be too fanciful to think that a growing boy may feel irritation to find himself 'crowded in' by another male in his own personal space. The fact that they are less "person orientated" than girls at an early age may well also be a corollary to this. The shared genetic make-up of identical boys may mask some of their need to stand apart but among adults twins, listing the disadvantages they could see in twinship, identical males most often said "I resented the lack of opportunity to be on my own".

Parents who answered the question, "What do you think your children got out of being twins?" seemed to confirm this suspicion. Parents of non-identical boys were the ones most likely to answer 'Not a lot' or 'Nothing as far as I can see'.

"I have twin boys aged ten," wrote one mother, "and they don't like each other at all. They don't even like walking down the road together."

Boy twins striving to be different were mentioned by several parents.

"My two at times seem to fall over each other to be different."

And adult twins looking back over their boyhood mentioned the efforts they had made to achieve some personal space.

"Me and my twin never got on when we were children. We were dressed alike but as we got older we would have territories in the house where the other could not go."

Some twin boys avoided closeness with their twin by teaming up with another member of the family which seemed to work very well and ease the tension.

"In our large family of three singles and two pairs of twins, the closest pairing is between the eldest boy and one of the non-identical twin boys."

And in another family of two sets, the closest pairings were across the sets, where the two from each pair who most closely resembled each other in appearance seemed to get on with each other best.

Not every pair of non-identical boys will be at each other's throats all the time but there does seem to be some evidence of an undercurrent of potential conflict between pairs of this type.

Parents have often found that parting this pair early can pay off.

"Mainly because our boys' sleep patterns are different, but also because they seemed keen they had different bedrooms from the age of three and a half," said one mother. "More often than not they are in each other's rooms but they seem to value the fact that they do have their own territory."

An adult twin considering whether twins might benefit from separation at school talked of his own experience of having been taught in a different class from his brother. Advocating separation, he said ". . . looking back I wonder now whether it might not have been better if we could have been sent to quite different schools altogether."

It looks as though different types of twins will react to their twinship in different ways. Girls would seem to be the most likely to enjoy closeness because it is likely to suit their temperament. Identical pairs are likely to enjoy it because their genetic similarity makes them less likely to be at odds, but the poor fraternal boy with neither zygocity nor gender in his favour seems the least likely to enjoy the idea of being a twin.

### But how about the boy/girl sets?

If difference in temperament does exist between boys and girls and if they are likely to develop at different rates, what can be said of the pairs who are boy/girl sets? Researchers, not surprisingly, find this pair intriguing. Helen Koch described the relationship between her boys/girls as, "Both more stimulating and more stressful" than that between her same sex pairs. "More stimulating" because the individual children tended to have wider interests than those in single sexed pairs, and "more stressful" because of an undercurrent of competition, not so evident between her single-sex pairs.

Talking of her own boy/girl twins, a mother describes almost exactly the relationship Helen Koch's research would lead one to expect.

"All their teachers remarked that there was a good deal of interest in what the other was doing and there was also a friendly rivalry between them . . . our son interested himself when very young in things like knitting and sewing while his sister was happy helping him with his boy's activities, woodwork, football and so on."

People are always curious as to how the proximity of young boy/girl twins will affect their future concept of gender, and this research with close siblings has uncovered some interesting facts. Boy/girl sibling pairs were found to influence each other's concepts of their boy's and girl's roles in unexpected ways. Boys with younger sisters showed more masculine traits when tested than other boys in a wider group of children. Girls with older brothers showed more feminine traits even than those with older sisters.

This boy with younger sister and the girl with the older brother are of course two sides of the same pair where the boy is older than the girl. In cases where the girl was older than the boy however things were different. This boy with the older sister was found to score lowest of all boys in tests of masculine characteristics. Having an older sister seemed to undermine the boy's concept of himself as a male, whereas having an older brother seems to enhance the girl's concept of herself as a female.

There was a nice sidelight to the picture of the boy with the older sister when the researchers turned to look at the boy with *two* older sisters; instead of any further decline, this boy's male rating had shot up to great heights. Perhaps parents, having at last produced a male child, made much of it, or perhaps it is just a case of the worm having turned!

It is quite easy to compare these brother/sister pairs with sets of boy/girl twins if we substitute 'stronger' for 'chronologically older'. Because of the dangerous circumstances of twin birth, the first born will not always be the stronger child. Baby boys are often more vulnerable at birth and therefore there will be as many pairs where girls take an early lead as their are pairs which are dominated by the boy.

Helen Koch was very interested in her group of mixed sex twins and she watched them as they started school. Her girls, she found, took the lead on social occasions in 81% of her pairs, and at the age of six the boys in these pairs were not happy with this role of follower.

This does not mean that these boys had not been quite happy to be led in the days before they came to school. A great deal of mothering is done by girl twins and this habit would not develop, one suspects, if the boys put up a strong resistance. After all, it is far easier to allow one's sister to do up your buttons than to bother to learn to do them up yourself. It is also much easier for a busy mother to allow or even to encourage this to happen, so at that time everyone was happy.

Some boys' dependence continues for much longer than this however. One girl remembered,

"I would do things like tying his shoes for him till he was eleven!"

At six years old these boy twins were the only ones to give Helen Koch a positive answer when asked whether they would like to change places with their twin, becoming by that the leader of the pair.

The girl who had a non-dependent brother on the other hand seemed to be quite happy to take the less assertive role. An adult twin related this directly to the sex of her twin when she said,

"He was more brainy than me—so he was put in a higher class—I didn't mind. If I had a twin sister though I'd have been annoyed if she was higher up."

The stronger sister in a mixed twin pair, despite appearing bossy and managing, can in fact feel uneasy if she is forced into the dominant role.

"Until puberty I was physically and mentally stronger and my childhood image of the dominant male was shattered. I always had to look after him whereas I saw my father was the one who looked after my mother—total confusion. Post teens we have become firm friends . . . Nature took control of the role playing and got it right, I no longer feel the need to be the dominant 'partner'."

Sometimes this changeover does not happen and once again we can hear the dissatisfaction of the girl twin forced into the stronger role.

"I am very independent. I'm sorry to say my twin is not. I find him irritating and he seems to be relying on me more and more e.g. to fill in an election form. He is not stupid or illiterate . . . He is a placid and cheerful person whose ambition is to win the pools."

There would seem to be a clear message for parents of mixed twin sets to intervene before unbalanced patterns become set. A bedroom of his own at an early age may give the less assertive boy some space to discover his abilities for himself, and as school approaches, separate classes are strongly indicated, as school presents an area where, as we have seen, his sister is almost certain to take the lead.

Reading and learning to read is the central focus of the first years at school and among five and six year olds the comparison of reading books is rife. In every playground some child is saying to another—

"I am on the Red Book. You must be stupid if you're still only on the Green one."

Knowing as we do that opposite sex twins are unlikely to progress at the same rate, it would be worth asking teachers, if they have to start in the same class, whether twins could follow separate schemes using different books so that such comparisons are not so instantly obvious.

By now we can see that if one were to make broad statements about the handling of twins it would mean that a great deal of advice would fall short of the mark. Identical reading schemes, for example, may do very well for one pair of twins, be ill advised for another and quite disastrous for a third.

This chapter has sorted out the general state of twinship into its five different groups so that any suggestions or advice may be better tailored to each twin type. Naturally there will be exceptions to every trend. Science doesn't tell us about individuals. It only traces general rules against which we can measure those who are exceptions.

# CHAPTER 9

# When twinship goes wrong

When we are well we are rarely aware of our physical state. It is when we are sick that the concept of health comes most clearly to mind. In the same way the patterns of relationship, both between twins, and evoked in us by twins, tend to be at their most apparent when something has gone wrong.

### The damaged pair

Twinship could be said to have gone wrong when one of a pair is born with a handicap. Sadly this is not an uncommon event. As we have seen earlier, the birth of twins is not without risk. Historically infant mortality among twins has been high. Today, with the help of advanced technology, many survive against the odds. Their lives are saved but not all are completely unscathed.

All parents of handicapped children grieve for what might have been. Parents of twins however have a daily living reminder of this 'might have been' running beside the wheelchair or romping ahead at school.

"I thought I had adjusted to it," said one mother," but Ben's first day at school was dreadful. Here was yet another reminder of something Gareth would never do."

As if the harsh realities of their situation were not enough, parents of twins are haunted by all of society's idealized concepts of twinship, and they mourn for both children the loss of what they feel ought to have been their birthright—perfect companionship. Parents themselves are also caught up in a special sense of loss. Speaking for many, one mother said, "I feel robbed. Especially now that they are older and Dan is still in the pushchair—I myself am no longer seen as a mother of twins."

The fact that outsiders no longer recognise that these twins are a pair does not diminish either the pressure of the pair effect on the parents or of the couple effect on the twins. Almost all parents of twins have a strong compulsion to balance an action towards one child with one of the same for the other. Where this is no longer appropriate the vacuum is filled by a feeling of guilt. One mother talking of her normal healthy toddlers explained:

"At breakfast my husband feeds one of the boys and I feed the other. David is the more active and he *will* wave his cup about. I am constantly telling him off. The other day I had been scolding him on and off when my husband said, 'Now say something to Daren'. I felt awful, for although the attention I had been giving David had been disapproving attention, I had been concentrating on him to the exclusion of the other twin."

In fact, attention from the father who was nearest and the parent most involved with Daren would have been quite enough to show his son that he was not being left out. But neither mother nor father saw the situation that way. Imagine a similar pressure at work on a mother whose twin has cystic fibrosis needing several hours of physiotherapy per day in order that he may breathe.

Other handicaps also require practical management specific to one twin. Cerebral palsy, one of the most common handicaps among twins, will often leave intelligence unimpaired but affect the mobility of the child. This twin will have to be lifted and carried by his mother for quite some time after the other one has learned how to walk.

Like many everyday actions, carrying has more to it than the simplest act of transport from A to B. As a child I remember 'having a carry' as a special treat. When my legs were small and I was tired, being carried meant that the adult took over the responsibility for getting to wherever we were going. It was also an added opportunity for extra cuddles. For little children, 'having a carry' symbolises their parents' love and care.

Where one twin is handicapped we tend to see as inevitable an overlap in time during which one can still be carried but where the other though now walking is still too young to understand quite why. "Carry *ME*! Carry *ME*!" This three-year-old's cry is no more anguished than his mother's despair that he is too young to be comforted by an explanation.

But is this the case? The pair effect can confuse us. As we still have a 'babe in arms' as it were must we still see the other as a baby too? In fact as we have seen twins are ready for communication much earlier than single children are, and many three-year-olds are capable of quite complex thought. Always explain—constantly, repetitively, even boringly—but do do it! Adult twins who have grown up with a handicapped partner tell us that it was years before they really understood what they saw as the preferential treatment of their twin.

It seems incredible that a child whose twin is disabled may not appreciate the fact. But disability to a child is merely difference. Adults are not seeing the minor inconvenience the stiff legs can cause their two-year-old today but envisaging the appalling handicap they will become to him in later life. Three, four, and five-year-olds do not suffer from such foresight. Even the six-year-old still regards being given a piggy back as a treat so how can 'having carrys' all the time be bad?

An engineer whose twin was born profoundly deaf remembers that it was only when his brother left for special school at seven that it began to dawn on him that he had some advantage that his brother lacked. Prior to this he had often been hurt and puzzled that attention focused so much on his twin. What had increased his bewilderment at first had been the fact that his brother's deafness had never prevented his communicating with him at all.

Explaining is not as easy as it sounds. Many parents are reluctant to talk of the future disadvantages awaiting the disabled child, within his hearing. In the case of twins who are rarely apart this may mean that clear explanation is never given to the well one at all. Many adult twins claimed no one had explained to them. This seems unlikely but what is certainly true is that no one seemed to have been able to explain to them successfully.

Twin children growing up together have always known their twins' disability. Their perception is not tinged with sadness for a might have been. Their attitudes are usually very accepting of the facts. Adjustments within a pair to even up the odds are more than possible if parents can help the well child understand the reasons for the unequal division of their (the parents') time. Horror that one twin has used the support of his brother's callipered leg to get a boost over the fence needs to be replaced by joy that they can co-operate in the adventure, and pointing out to the disabled one that his crutch is just the right length to poke the ball out of the tree is a triumph on the part of twins' parents.

This would be a triumph because so much is stacked up against their acquiring such an attitude. The strong traditional bias of protection towards the handicapped child needs much closer examination in the case of twins. We need to know that well twins have often been deeply jealous of their partners' access to special swimming lessons and to riding for the disabled. But many parents are reluctant to encourage the equivalent classes for them for fear of emphasising the ability gap that yawns between them.

But the well twin who feels deprived will take his own way to get attention. Dr Elizabeth Bryan in her book *Twins In The Family* writes of some of these reactions she had observed. There were twins who became withdrawn and others who developed symptoms mimicking those which handicapped their twins. There were many who just produced some difficult behaviour to ensure that somebody noticed them.

"Tom demands so much attention," said one mother. "People used to say to me, how difficult it must be to have a handicapped child but once I understood Sean's treatment that was no trouble. Tom was the one who never kept still. I have never had a night's sleep with him and yet they say at school he is good as gold." With his brother asleep Tom had discovered his own way of making up for the times he was unable to get his mother to himself.

Professionals could help here in some small ways. Parents of handicapped children spend the first five years and more in an endless round of visits to clinics. There are doctors, physiotherapists, speech therapists, teachers and psychologists to be seen. Where there is a pair transport and childminding is a problem, so the twin usually comes too. People who appreciate that the child they are seeing is a twin should look round for the well partner and acknowledge his presence. Physiotherapists could gain ground by making exercises into a game for both children. Speech therapists can also enlist the help of this constant companion and give him a sense of importance instead of allowing him to feel like a second-class citizen because no one wants to see his teeth or tongue. The proximity of this well twin can be an asset to his handicapped partner if the adults around him will make the effort to avoid his alienation.

It seems very hard that parents already coping with the

problems of disability may also be saddled with behaviour difficulties within the pair. Who can help? In Britain and Australia the Multiple Births Association hold voluntary registers of parents of twins where one or both have special needs. Following their belief that mutual support is often the best they put parents in touch with each other where problems seem the same. Even sharing tips and general information can be a help but the overwhelming relief reported by most parents who join this postal contact service is the discovery that they are not alone, and that the behaviour they are seeing is not bizarre but part of the pattern of normal twinship at large.

## The damaged bond

Human psychology seems to be programmed for pairing. Every single person is a potential partner in a monogamous marriage. 'Two is company, three's a crowd' is making some sort of statement which we all understand. It would seem however that in a family where there are two pairings, father, mother, twin, twin, care may need to be taken to make sure that these alignments stay the same. Earlier the pair effect has been discussed almost exclusively in a critical light. There is a possibility however that it may be present in our makeup as a protection against destructive interaction across these pairs.

In families where things go wrong there are times when the dynamics of the married couple's interaction may be mirrored by the twins. An identical girl said,

"We had a very unhappy childhood; my twin and I have never been close but this was mainly because we sided with opposite parents when they rowed and I think it has always left a mark on me."

The girl of a boy/girl pair deeply regretted a similar situation in her family: "I longed to get on better with my brother, and still do, but he can never forgive me for having taken my father's part in the endless matrimonial battles. It's as if we too were now divorced."

Marital upsets will often split a family but in the case of twins there is a danger that the line of division may have already been laid down. Early photographs in the family album often show proud parents each holding one baby. In some cases a quick leaf through the pages shows the same baby always held by the same parent. This can of course arise through the natural affinity between one parent and one child, as even in infancy temperamental differences are quite marked. It is also quite common that at first the cry of one child sets the mother on edge but doesn't bother the father. This phase of preference usually disappears as infant wails die down, but the pattern of care by one parent rather than the other can persist as a habit. Most parents are quick to notice when this happens and a conscious change is made so both can get to know each child equally well.

Unfortunately, however, the early days of infant care are the ones most likely to put a strain on a marriage, so any arrangement which will ease the running of the household is quite likely to be allowed to continue, for fear of rocking the boat. Later, however, the children may find it easy to read preference into what has genuinely begun as a practical arrangement.

Pressure on either of these two partnerships is now set fair to exert equal stress on the other. One parent's ambition for 'his' or 'her' twin may lead to dissent between the parents. Splitting the twins from each other in this case may have the same effect on the marriage as we have seen that the break-up of the parents has on them.

"My sister was called 'Daddy's Girl' and I was called 'Mummy's Girl'—in a family where twins are the only children I think it is important to avoid each parent favouring one, particularly where the marriage is a bit shaky as it was in our case."

At the dawn of history one of the most famous stories of conflict between twins had parent preference as its background. This lesson has been there in the Bible for centuries ready for us to learn:

Late in life Rebecca, Isaac's wife, had non-identical twin sons whom they called Jacob and Esau. The story of their birth and how their mother encouraged her younger son Jacob to deceive his father into giving him his brother's birthright is found in *Genesis* chapters 26–28. The lengths to which Jacob later went to try to repair his relationship with Esau, after their mother's death, are also worth looking at in chapter 32.

What concerns us here however is the statement right at the beginning of the story which sets the scene for the intrigue that followed:

"And the boys grew: Esau was a cunning hunter, a man of the field; and Jacob was a plain man living in tents. And Isaac loved Esau, because he did eat of his venison—but Rebecca loved Jacob."

As in classical mythology the stories of the Bible outline all the possible elements of distortion in family relationships which psychology today is only just beginning to map out. What psychology can do for us is to pinpoint factors which may start off as harmless arrangements and warn us against their potentially destructive future power.


### Damage to the supportive environment

Where the duo does not split it can generate its own energy for protection against invasive forces. This was what Kuluchova discovered in the twins boys locked in the cellar. But there are times when this potential power within a pair confined neither by lock and key nor by the normal controls and disciplines of family life can develop along sinister lines. The instinctive tendency to close ranks against an outside threat can begin to take over to the point where it is the pair who pose the threat to others and no outside threat is there at all.

Reginald and Ronald Kray, the notorious twins who violently dominated London's gangland during the fifties, grew up in a highly delinquent culture. Their rise to power is documented by John Pearson in his book *The Profession of Violence*. Given the background he describes it is fairly likely that the twins would have embarked on a life of crime even had they been born apart. Their twinship did not trigger their delinquency. It did however help to ensure its 'success'.

Having been able to fight as two against one when young, they discovered and exploited this power that is inherent in all pairs. The balance within their partnership was not merely that of two synchronized 'heavies'. The couple effect was at work for them too. Their strength came from the stability induced within the twinship by the better administrator who carefully compensated for the excesses of his more flamboyant twin. Colleagues in crime could approach one if the other was being unreasonable. One rarely failed to support the other despite marked personality differences which, as in the case of the original siamese twins, increased with age.

The destructive force of this twinship is made efficient by the degree of control the twins exert upon each other. In the one case this is to preserve the partnership in operation in relation to those outside it. On the other it is to tighten the bond against partition of the pair. The 'quieter twin' having learned fairly early to manage the partnership on behalf of them both has probably acquired sufficient social skill to stand alone if need be. Separation for him is still feared with the apprehension we all have of the unknown. For the 'stronger' partner who has not had to develop internal controls separation may seem to threaten loss of support and even the disintegration of the self. The tie of twinship tightens as a result of emotional blackmail and suicide threats, which are doubly effective as either twin without the other implies the loss of the dual identity for ever.

This rather than their decision not to speak was the sort of complicated tangle which developed between Jennifer and June Gibbons, often called the 'silent twins'. Marjorie Wallace who told the world their story in her book entitled *The Silent Twins* wrote:

"June and Jennifer . . . two human beings who love and hate each other with such intensity that they can neither live together nor apart . . . If they come too close or drift apart, both are destroyed. So the girls devised games and strategies and rules to maintain this equilibrium."

One of these rules was not to be the first to speak to adults, but as each closely monitored the other this soon meant that neither spoke to anyone except her twin, a school friend, and a younger sister. Keeping this up cut them off from the realities of normal life and led to a series of tragic incidents ending in a spate of fire-raising. For this they were committed to Broadmoor Hospital in 1982 aged nineteen years.

Problems with speech are not uncommon in twins and even total mutism is not unknown. It is important to appreciate however that it was not lack of speech which led to things going wrong for the Gibbons girls. In the north, a pair of ten-year-old identical twin boys speak clearly but with totally different accents. Each has retained the intonation of his individual speech therapist. Up to the age of four neither had uttered a single audible sound but they were neither deaf nor suffered from any serious impediment. Between them they had an elaborate sign language not based on mime and therefore a closed book to outsiders. When their mother invited other children in to play with them in the hope that they might encourage the boys to speak she found to her dismay that instead the other children picked up the sign language and all games were played in silence.

From the first signs of trouble their mother searched for help and at last when they were nearly five intensive speech therapy did the trick. Quite opposite to the Gibbons who were refusing to communicate these boys could not wait to learn and would rush to the door to welcome their therapists. Mutism was clearly a problem and a frustration to them and by no means a matter of choice.

There is however a lesson to be learnt from the story of the silent twins. Although they had had several changes of primary school, it does seem strange that these little girls, who were developing a dangerous and sinister relationship, were not picked up as giving cause for concern until their second year in secondary school. There was some early attempt at speech therapy but because they refused to co-operate this was abandoned. A visiting medical officer giving TB vaccinations at the school was the one to pick them up not, interestingly enough, because of their lack of speech but because of an oddity of manner which filled him with unease.

The one feature of children who do not talk is that they are quiet and in a class of thirty, quiet children are seen as good and not noticed unless their written work is poor. Jennifer and June had a good grasp of language and their written work was fine, so their quietly odd behaviour was not seen as needing help. It is possible that as the only West Indian children in the Welsh school any aberrations might have been put down to cultural difference. Nevertheless, from reading one of the comments this does seem rather unlikely.

"One day I was in with the school secretary whose window looks out onto the playground," says Cyril Dabis, their head-master, "and there were the twins doing a kind of goosestep, walking ten yards one behind the other very slowly as though in some kind of stately procession. 'Do they always walk like that?' I asked the secretary. 'Yes,' she said. I couldn't believe it and jumped in my car to see how long they would keep it up. I followed them through the town, still doing their dead march, one following the other." This was nothing to do with their being from another culture, nor as they were unaware that they were being observed was it directed at outsiders. This was the power of one twin being exerted on the other to keep in line and obey rules which had been laid down.

From this it is clear that schools need co-operation from home and home from school in order to pinpoint and treat any early problems. It is also clear that twinship itself rather like another culture may be regarded as likely to produce oddities in a pair which may be brushed off. As in the case of the silent twins, such things may be ignored to their cost.

This chapter has concentrated on the few occasions where twinship has gone wrong. Most twins grow up in a normal, happy environment but even there we still find things to learn. In the first part of this book research has provided us with a framework of rather cold facts. Now, in the second part, twins themselves help us to complete the picture by filling it in from their memories and giving it life through the colour and variety of their personal experience.

# PART II

# *What do twins themselves have to say?*

## CHAPTER 10

# A survey of six hundred

This survey asked adult twins and parents of adult twins to answer questions to give a picture of their experience of children growing up in partnership. Postal questionnaires were backed by interviews and by group discussions. Most of those who took part answered a letter published in the *Observer* newspaper, the *Daily Express*, or *Woman* magazine, or wrote in after hearing about it on local radio stations.

A general survey like this does have some drawbacks. This method of collecting information may attract only those who feel strongly. Twins who had hated being twins might write because they had an axe to grind; those who had loved their twinship might over-state their praise of it. There was a risk that the response would be weighted at these extremes and weak on the experience of the average child, which was our main interest.

As it turned out, the very fact of being a twin was seen to be sufficiently different in itself to motivate parents and twins to feel that even the mildest comment on their experience would be worth making. There were, in fact, very few letters which fell into the extreme categories and it was clear that in most of these cases other factors had been at work in the family relationships which had caused twinship to become either a focus of unhappiness or grounds for special pleading.

A simple example of this came from identical twin girls, brought up abroad, who felt very strongly on the subject of identical dressing. They went on to say that their other sisters were also dressed like them because their mother had had a bolt of cloth sent out from England each summer from which dresses were made for the entire family. Their feeling about being dressed alike had therefore been influenced by more than just their own twinship and was not felt to be quite representative of the feelings of twins in general.

The questionnaire which was sent out was a fairly simple one.

It was accompanied by a letter encouraging those taking part to ignore the questions if they found them inappropriate and to write instead about their own experience. The response was overwhelming. Many people ignored the questions altogether and sent in essays on their childhood. It was also common to have questionnaires returned with more writing on the back than on the pages where the questions were typed. 597 questionnaires were filled in and returned. They were then augumented by over thirty interviews, bringing the number of twin and twin parent participants to 600 in all. The overall impression gained from the volume of replies from the twins in particular was that one had tapped an enormous group of people who had at last been offered an opportunity to express some of the things they had been mulling over in their minds for years. Twins tended to ask as many questions as they answered. Zygocity and heredity were the areas which had confused them most but all the old rumours of myth, magic and mystery which have always surrounded the idea of twinship had their mention too.

As the forms were returned they were filed by zygocity and sex into the five pair groups and it soon became apparent that this survey like all other twin surveys was going to be affected by an uneven spread. Where the subjects are volunteers rather than carefully counted groups chosen from a register, twin samples almost always end up with a preponderance of identical girls. This is usually followed by another large group of fraternal girls and a slightly smaller group of boy/girl pairs. Some identical males will be sufficiently interested in their special genetic make-up to take part but fraternal boys with no particular spur to make them take an interest are the twins least likely to be represented. This pattern ties in almost exactly with what was said in the previous chapter about the degree to which the different groups take pleasure in their twinship.

Almost three times as many identical as fraternal girls took part in this survey and that was almost five times the number of fraternal boys who became involved. Between these extremes came the boy/girl pairs with the same number of replies as the fraternal girls—perhaps because two thirds of their forms were filled in by the girl partner. The small number of identical males who took part was only slightly greater than the number of non-identical males who replied.

*Actual Numbers of Twins and Parents of Twins taking part in the Survey*

|                     | Adults | Total | Mothers |
|---------------------|--------|-------|---------|
| Identical Boys      | 29     | 80    | 51      |
| Non Identical Boys  | 20     | 47    | 27      |
| Boy Girl Sets       | 62     | 132   | 70      |
| Identical Girls     | 157    | 213   | 56      |
| Non Identical Girls | 80     | 127   | 47      |

Groups in a general sample must be of a reasonable size if they are to show up trends. It was therefore essential to top up this small male group. Using the fact that a penchant for form filling is one of those traits which is to be found at the feminine end of a personality scale, the questionnaire for parents of twins was addressed to the mothers and in this way the information on twin boys was topped up to a usable size.

The spread of parents' responses was also interesting. In spite of the huge response from identical girls the number of identical girls' *mothers* who replied was not significantly large. This would seem to imply that the daughters' interest in their twinship was not merely a reflection of their mothers' pride in them, but something quite specific to the twins themselves.

Among the parent group, mothers of mixed sex sets were the most motivated to take part. This was interesting considering the widespread impression that boy/girl twinships have little significance beyond their pre-school years. It may also link up with Helen Koch's finding that this pairing was the 'most stimulating and most stressful' so that parents of boy/girl pairs may have had more to write about.

There were twice as many replies from mothers of identical sets which may reflect the special pride parents have in identical twins, than from mothers of fraternal sets. It may also indicate that fraternal boys are not so difficult to bring up and so give one little to comment about if one allows the fact of their twinship to be more or less ignored.

Several twins and parents of twins volunteered to be interviewed in order to fill out the picture which came out of the written replies. Where twins were interviewed together it was often fascinating to see their relationship being acted out before one's eyes as they tried to describe it in words. Interviews with one parent and one twin were also interesting as both could fill in for the other their side of incidents which had involved the absent twin. This often made up a picture which an interview with one alone would not have been able to invoke. Sometimes this filled in minor aspects of the relationship between the twins but in one instance there was something more.

One mother of twin daughters away from home at different universities had been in the habit of keeping in touch with them by phone. Both rang up one evening, one after the other. The first mentioned among other things, that she had had a terrifying nightmare about someone shining a bright light in her eyes like the interrogator in a spy film. When the other daughter phoned, she told her mother that she had had a terrible fright the night before when her flatmate, coming home from a party at three in the morning had switched the light on suddenly making her wake with a start. The daughter at the interview had never heard this side of her mother's conversation before so that talking to them together had added another dimension to an almost forgotten incident.

Finding the right questions to ask in interviews and on the questionnaire presented a major difficulty. Because I am a single born person I may be quite unaware of whole areas of experience which exist for twins. They, on the other hand, might be equally unaware that some of their experiences are not common to those who are not twins. One pair of siamese twins who had been separated at birth told, for example, that they had always assumed that a private language like the one they had shared until their teens was common among all children in all families. It had not occurred to them to mention it to their friends as they had assumed that they too communicated with their brothers and sisters in this fashion.

In an effort to bring such differences to the surface, several groups of twins agreed to meet together to talk about their twinship between themselves while I observed. One of the results of this was that a group of teenagers confirmed that twin children are more than usually anxious about the physical safety of their partner. Members of this group acknowledged an actual concern about how they themselves would survive were their twin to die or disappear. This was discussed as something strongly felt and understood by other twins, even by pairs whom an observer might have been led to suspect felt little love for each other.

The group of sixteen-year-olds who discussed this had already tried to envisage what it would be like to live on if their twin should suddenly die. This is not something that is often forced upon a single child in relation to his siblings, although some may perform a similar self-examination exercise trying to imagine how they would cope were their mother to die. Both activities are about testing the strength of a relationship and of gauging for oneself exactly how one stands.

These discussion groups were used to test out some of the questions which might be asked in the questionnaire but the majority of these had been suggested by the areas which I already knew parents had found to be difficult or phases to which they looked forward with apprehension. Adolescence featured most often here, the difficulty most often foreseen being how to help and encourage one twin where the other was having more success with the opposite sex.

Some questions were included to test unproved theories and it was just as productive to have one exploded by the questionnaire replies than to have another confirmed. There is for example a suggestion that a demanding baby will develop into a dominant child, but according to the replies of the parents in this survey it is not necessarily borne out where the children are twins.

Another supposition which had been thought to be solely negative was shown in some cases to have a positive side as well. One of the twins in a pair who study the same subject at school will sometimes refuse to continue to compete if their twin begins to do better. As expected, some twins remembered making such a decision in bitter frustration, but others had seen their decision to stop trying in that subject as a release from a pointless self-imposed pressure to keep level. Where, on the one side, the refusal to do any work in the subject had been negative and resentful, the second response can be a mature method of coming to terms with a real state of affairs. The questionnaire often invoked more than the questioner had thought to be there.

Because these question are open-ended, they are necessarily an inaccurate tool for measurement. Not everyone answered all the questions and not all questions applied to every twin. It would be pointless, for example, to list 100 twins out of 600 as objecting to having to wear name badges at school. Some would have had no need to do so, having attended different schools, but their answer including this reason would not have been clear. Quoting statistics from the survey has therefore been kept to a minimum. It has rather been left to the reader to judge for himself if a pattern of findings is emerging which might be significant.

The questionnaire forms were anonymous but several people chose to write their names on them. In order to preserve privacy all names have been changed and situations revised while still retaining the sense of the stories. Sometimes, the separate forms of two twins were identifiable and could be matched up. As two halves of the same experience they were often fascinating. The purpose of the survey was, however, to try to elicit what it had been like for each individual to be brought up as a twin, and as on almost every form there was a plea that twins be allowed to be seen as individuals, it seemed that participants were in agreement with the aim.

The age of twins taking part in this survey had originally been set at over eighteen as it was felt that beyond that age one might be less affected by feelings of betrayal if the answers to some questions meant implying criticism of one's parents or of one's twin. It became clear, however, that in the case of parents the day to day problems of child rearing had happily been dimmed by time. To balance this gift of amnesia that nature had so wisely handed out several younger teenage twins and their parents were also interviewed.

At the upper end of the age scale, several forms were received from twins in their seventies and even some in their eighties. Their memories gave a marvellous insight into the enormous changes that have occurred in childcare and in our concept of parenthood. Where twinship was concerned, however, the strong views held by society in their young days were much the same as those still encountered today, emphasising yet again our need to know more on the subject.

Already armed with a general scientific background to twinship from the previous chapters, the experience of these individual twins and their parents should help us fill in the gaps in our knowledge of what it is like to travel through childhood as 'one of a pair'.

# CHAPTER 11

# *Double benefits*

Two questions helped us gain a general impression of twinship. Twins were asked:

"What do you think of as the good things about being a twin?" and that was balanced by another question,

"What sorts of things, if any, made you wish you had never been born a twin?"

The overwhelming majority of twins in this survey regarded their twinship as something positive which had enriched their lives. Those who had had reservations were also able to enter items on the credit side. Even when the question itself presented difficulties, the answer given was a positive one.

"Not having been anything else (but a twin) I have a problem answering these questions but I can say it suited me fine!"

Out of 345 adult twins who answered this first question only four had felt that they gained nothing at all from their twinship. Three others felt that it was just like having another brother or sister, but even one who had shown elsewhere in her questionnaire that she had not enjoyed being a twin, was able to write—"I suppose it can be fun sometimes."

The twins listed advantages under two main headings. Those shared by the partners within the twinship like 'the joy of having someone special to you', and those which arose by virtue of being one of a unit of two, like 'having access to one's twin's friends as well as one's own'.

## Two's company

Companionship was seen as the main advantage by almost a third of twins and their parents. "A ready-made best friend"—"We had a fun childhood"—or "You always had someone to play with," expressed this but the most valuable aspect of twinship for many was that this compatability had continued on into adult life.

"We have an extreme closeness as adults, without living in each other's pockets," explained one twin. Another agreed saying,

"We lead very different lives now but we remain emotionally very close."

## Having someone who is special to you

The general companionship of spaced siblings had been enriched into something different for some twins.

"Being best friends as well as sisters," expressed this for one pair but others wanted to go further in describing what they felt.

"I think whatever happened in the world I would always have my sister to turn to if my parents were no longer there."

"I think the importance of being a twin is that you know that there is always another half out there belonging to you and you must look after it."

"Someone you know will never just leave you . . . you can go anywhere in the world for as long as you like and you know your twin will always be there to come back to."

The girl of a boy/girl pair expressed this as, "Constant friendship, even after marriage—the pleasure I get from seeing him again."

A comparison of the feelings one had for one's other siblings sometimes helped to pinpoint what was felt for a twin.

"Out of our family which had split badly we are the only two who have stayed close."

"I can't think of any specific things that stemmed from our being twins having shared my brother with our other two sisters, but an intense pride in having a twin brother has persisted all my life."

## Having a confidant

The essence of this special companionship for some twins was being able to exchange confidences. Most remembered this as an invaluable support during adolescence.

"Being able to share very intimate secrets and guilts," had been the best thing for one twin.

"Being with somewho who is going through the same things at the same time—eg exams, meeting members of the opposite sex, leaving home—a good chance to discuss things," said another.

Others expressed the same thing as, "Always having someone to talk to and be honest with," or "Always someone to confide in and someone to argue with."


### Having an unspoken understanding

Many twins felt there was an added depth to this exchange of confidences. Some explained it in practical terms.

"Knowing there will always be someone who shared your early experiences—it means that so much does not have to be said."

"As adults—knowing your twin will always understand . . . share happiness and sorrow without needing long explanations."

What is interesting is not so much that the twins did not need to have long explanations but their assumption that other folk would have needed them. This brings back an echo from the earlier chapter on communication.

"Never having to explain at length—having no reservations whatsoever."

"Never having to say much because your other half understood."

Married couples or close friends must experience something similar when a shared memory is evoked by a look or gesture, but few would claim to have experienced the same degree of mutual understanding as the twins who said that what they valued was:

"Being able to say whatever you like without having to think of her reaction first."

This mutual acceptance of whatever each may throw at the other was expressed again and again. Another aspect of the same thing was described as,

"Never having to apologise after a fight."

It is difficult for those of us who are single born to grasp what is being said here. An elderly twin was probably expressing a similar thought when she said,

"We never kiss each other as it would be silly, like kissing yourself."

It was interesting to note that twins who gave these answers were not necessarily those who gave positive answers to later questions on telepathy. What was being described here was not something that they had found to be unusual but rather a part of normal experience of everyday life with their twin.

"My twin and I work as plasterers, and we never have to think what the other is doing because we just know—we sense."

### Practical advantages of operating as a pair

Not all the advantages of being twins are on deep levels. Practical considerations featured near the top of most people's lists of advantages.

"Two to help with the washing up!"—"You can borrow clothes, borrow money. Great!"

Being able to share homework was remembered by several as a very definite bonus and as we will see in a later chapter this was often exactly what they did, each doing for the other the bit he or she did best.

### A partner for sport

"Always having a partner for games—if she'll co-operate," was mentioned by several twins reminding us of the high proportion, particularly of identical twins, who participate in sport world-wide. Britain's Fudge twins pacing for each other in training until they were of Olympic standard, and Canada's pentathlon twins doing the same, are examples of how similarity of interest and physique help spur a pair on to greater and greater prowess in sport.

"If she'll co-operate" is however a significant rider here as only those pairs who get on well together will both reach these heights. Prowess in sport may also come out of twinship for one twin but the dynamics of the effort may be fuelled by rivalry or resentment. The mother of one successful international runner said,

"I do believe it is a driving force to do better than his brother that had made him so determined."

*Competition*

Surprisingly, several twins and their parents valued competitiveness as a bonus for twins. As we saw earlier one twin felt that having had someone to argue with was just as much of an advantage as having had someone in whom to confide. Another who had listed the main advantage as "A constant playmate and close friend" went on to say "Mind you, when we were young we had dreadful fights, hair pulling and biting each other."

Perhaps this overt behaviour which can look potentially damaging to the future relationship of children is in fact a necessary safety valve to those who are emotionally so close.

"Too much tends to be made of quarrels between twin children," said a social worker, a twin himself, and who had had several twin boys in his care. "They are not always what they seem."

One of the girls gave a good example of the contrast between her mother's memory of their childhood and her actual feelings for her twin at the time, when she said,

"According to my mother we quarrelled every day . . . I used to beat him up . . . We always stuck up for each other and ganged up on anyone else. I was always protective towards him, maybe it was because he was the smaller and always ill."

Competition need not necessarily imply argument and aggression. Parents who mentioned the positive effects of competition in the survey were usually referring to schoolwork.

"Competing against each other helped them academically."

"There was friendly rivalry, both their standards were high, if one was first this time, then the other would be next time."

This, of course, will only work for twins who have an equal chance of success.

*Presenting a united front*

Although competition did exist, the luxury of being able to retire behind a united front in the face of outside opposition had been a great asset for many in childhood. Schools which parents tend to think of as classrooms only, have their playgrounds too.

"You always had an ally in the playground." "We stuck up for each other, covered for each other," said the girl of one girl/boy pair.

"He always helped me sort out other children when they used to fight me, which was quite often as I had a quick temper."

As a pair twins can be formidable allies. Sometimes the threat from outside was the unfamiliarity of situations. Then it was reassuring to have a twin on hand.

"Always having someone with you when starting at a school or club," was an advantage for most twins. Parents who had perhaps dreaded a double scene at the dentist or on the first day at school, remember having benefited from this aspect of twinship too.

"Difficult situations seemed to have less impact on the twins. We noticed this in comparison to our third son's reaction to his first day at the dentist and then again on his first day at school."

This mutual support has another side to it however.

"They got moral support from each other in social situations but they both suffer from shyness which their older brother never did."

Twins themselves acknowledge this.

"At parties you had someone to go with, it's more of a worry going by yourself."

## Twinship in the family

Twins remembered their support for each other when they had to face the outside world, but some pairs remembered this mutual support as having been useful in the family setting too.

"My twin was my support and comfort in our sad upbringing."

We have seen earlier how their twinship can give protection to children in unhappy surroundings but even having support in ordinary family arguments was felt to have been one of the good things about being a twin. Parents sometimes referred to this as the twins 'ganging up' on them but most twins had used it in much more subtle ways.

Two pairs explained how they would sort out which of them was currently most in favour with their parents before asking for some privilege. They would also take advantage of the fact that their parents' perception of them was as a pair.

"We would be allowed to go more places because there were two of us."

"We often used to go out together in our teens, therefore Mum and Dad did not worry so much because we were not alone."

## Being special

Another more obvious aspect of having each other to go out with was that,

"You always have someone to go shopping with . . . if nobody else can go with you."

And when they were out together,

"Always being noticed"—was fun for many twins.

One identical boy who described his being a twin as "the biggest non-event of my life" conceded that despite that he did enjoy "belonging to a small unpersecuted minority—an elite!"

It was not only the identical twins who attracted attention however. A fraternal girl said,

"People are always interested in us. It is something to tell people. It's quite unusual."

Twins who did enjoy the attention they attracted revelled in it.

"I relish the occasions when we enjoy the limelight!"

One mother said,

"When they complain about each other's faults being reflected unfairly I would remind them it was a small price to pay for the charisma that surrounded them."

For some twins this attention which they get from outsiders heightens their awareness of what they share together and intensifies the feeling that the reason they are special is "because of each other".

## Being popular

Twins who got on well together attracted other people by their élan. Many of the twins in this survey had been popular at school. Helen Koch had also found this to be the case among her group of six-year-olds in Chicago. The twins who said,

"We have such fun . . . we find it an asset making friends. People are always intrested in us," spoke for many.

"We were able to play tricks on teachers and friends and still keep on having lots of friends."

Twins who enjoyed this popularity with their peers were often those who felt most secure within their partnerships. It may even have been this assurance which was attractive to others.

"It may sound smug, but neither of us needed anybody else," said one very outgoing pair.

Parents had often observed this self-absorption of twins with each other in their pre-school years. One mother recalls her boy/girl pair completely ignoring friends who had come to play, another dreaded their being asked to play at friends' houses as she knew once they got there they only played together. Later at school in separate classes, both pairs developed other friendships in the normal way but their central attachment was still to each other even on into adulthood.

Twins expressed this stability within their partnership as,

"Never being lonely"—"I was never alone up till the age of eighteen."

But one mother who described herself as being elderly pointed out another side to this:

"They are so used to being together they are always looking for company and don't enjoy the benefits of solitude, they are always bothering me and saying—'will you be all right on your own this evening?'—They can't seem to understand that I love it!"

Feeling lonely is, of course, a different matter from being alone. For some, twinship can bring the emotional reassurance of attachment which does not need to be reinforced by the partner's physical presence.

"My husband and I were only children and were delighted to have two at once, it must be great to have a friend. However, we feel as they do that times spent apart are valuable; both of them agree that they like to be on their own for a bit but the reunions after separation are touching."

However, because practical arrangements tend to reinforce twins' attachment to each other, both parents and twins felt them to be assets. Things like shared bed times and bath times, appeared on the list. Even questionable advantages like being ill together got a mention.

"It's great to have someone to talk to if you have been sent to bed early!"

"It's an advantage to have someone to cuddle through the night."

*The possession of a dual identity*

The continued proximity of twins throughout childhood can develop a dual identity for the pair. For many twins, this central feature of their relationship summed up all the other advantages in one.

"It's always having the choice of being either half of a couple or of being a single person."

"It's having dual identity—one's own individuality and also the identity that goes with the pair."

Because this idea is new and difficult for single born people to grasp, it has been overlooked. Single born people tend to perceive being part of a pair, and having individual identity as mutually exclusive, whereas these adult twins are saying that they run parallel, and that the one can enrich the other.

Young twins probably start off with a strong 'pair' image and then move on to discover that they possess individual indentity too. Where on the one hand, those involved with twins must resist the temptation to see them as a unit of two, denying the existence of 'pair identity' can be a mistake too. If, as in one case, it has been decided that twins might benefit from separation in school, it could be unwise to make a clean sweep at home as well and put them into separate bedrooms at that time too. Such a combined assault on the pair identity of one set of twins defeated the object of the exercise and produced instead of independence, a defensive shrinking together which made their original problem worse.

It is always easier to see the disadvantages in a situation than to appreciate the inherent benefits which may be disturbed by any change. Discussions of twin development often overlook the advantages of twinship which we have been considering in this chapter, but should we be ready to jettison all this in the pursuit of an exclusive concept of individuality, just because that is the only thing that we, in our single state, can understand? Somewhere a balance can be struck which will not deny twin children access to what is after all their birthright.

"In my twin", said one adult, "I have a friend for life, and although I think it may be said we hindered each other's independence, it is also true that we benefit from having two views of life, two sets of friends, and that we personally reap the benefits of each other's separate experience."

No wonder we singletons watching from the sidelines when these twins count their blessings, catch ourselves saying "Twins, how nice!"

# CHAPTER 12

# Dual disadvantage

After a chapter recommending twinship what, one may ask, can possibly go wrong? The majority of twins would in fact echo this. When those in the survey were asked, "What things make you wish you had never been a twin?" many replied,

"Nothing nearly as strong as never—the rewards overwhelm any such difficulties."

Despite this, some things were listed on the debit side. They ranged from the mild embarrassment of the teenage boy/girl pair who said, "People keep thinking we are going out with each other," and the universally acclaimed disadvantage of having to share one's birthday, to an impassioned plea that the very word 'twin' should be expunged from the language altogether.

"Why can't we just be treated as two children of the same age?—I can rarely ever remember *not* wishing that I was not a twin," said one fraternal girl.

Some of the main difficulties of twinship arise between the members of the pair.

"When you feel as opposite to a person as I do, it can only irritate." But problems also originate outside the partnership.

"There was a pressure on us to act like people think twins ought to act instead of letting us lead our own lives."

*Dealing with society's ignorance*

Most twins found it difficult to explain their twin status to outsiders.

"We hated people saying, 'What is it like to be a twin?'—How do I know, I have never been anything else."

When they had tried to explain, their explanations had often been challenged.

"People ask—'Are you identical?'—and then say 'But your hair is lighter.'"

"At infant school, different hair ribbons were taken to mean we were not identical."

Even as adults, twins found this difficult to deal with.

"At work when I say I am a twin, people expect to see a twin appear out of nowhere or expect to see one growing out of my side. I hate being treated like a freak."

And yet, outsiders ask these questions out of genuine interest and not with the intention of embarrassing the twin in any way.

Twins will always be asked about their twinship. Identical pairs are the most likely to be questioned but the fraternal set are the more likely to have their answers challenged. The little girls with different ribbons were upset to be denied their special status but at least their facial similarity would have borne out their claim.

Parents need to support twins by making sure they have some sort of answer ready so they need not squirm in embarrassment. If they are old enough to understand their own origin, they may get a kick out of being better informed than their questioner. Some twins have found other ways to turn the question,

"Our brother used to say, 'yes they are twins—there was a litter but the rest were drowned!'"

*Why are they staring?*

Questions about twinship were not the only attentions twins resented.

"People almost took bets on which was which—that made us very shy and unsociable and forced us to seek each other's company."

Disturbingly, this attention had been totally misunderstood by many twins when they were young.

". . . we were not aware why people stared. It was only when we were apart that they stopped staring."

". . . I thought it was because we were peculiar ie ugly—it was lovely to go out on my own and not be stared at."

It may be difficult to believe that identical twins, in particular, do not always understand why people stare at them. Parents who have been stopped in the street by the exclamations of passers-by since they were born tend to assume that the children must have come to understand what it is all about. It seems from the survey that one would be quite wrong to make that assumption.

Even adult identical twins said that they found it genuinely difficult to believe that people were unable to tell them apart. Some, who were in fact indistinguishable, were convinced that they were not alike at all. It was only when they themselves met another identical set at medical school, that one pair of twin doctors had realised why others had had such difficulty in telling them apart.

As outsiders, we are immediately aware of 'the pair', whereas each individual twin only ever sees the other twin as one. Their double image in the mirror or on a photograph does not have this same 'pair' effect on them. When we look at a photograph of someone else's family what we notice first is the composition of the picture as a whole but if we, ourselves, feature in it, it is our own image which will attract us first. Each twin, too, checks to see how they have turned out and so they do not instantly respond to themselves as 'a pair' even in photographs where they do see themselves together.

Not being able to appreciate quite why people are staring at them, many twins feel resentful. Some had their own way of dealing with other people's rudeness. Twin girls brought up in Paris remembered being the focus of all eyes as they travelled on the underground.

"We would wait till we had them all gawping at us then at a signal between us we would simultaneously proceed to pull the most grotesque grimaces we could muster."

But not all children were so confident. Another twin remembers,

"I grew up with an inferiority complex through people staring at us every time we went out. I felt like a thing and not a person."

It is dangerous to assume that the children understand why people stare at them. If they do not know the real reason they will substitute their own. Parents can fairly easily turn what can be an unhappy misunderstanding into a secret boost for the morale. Little ones may quite enjoy the idea that they are like the Royal Family in that they attract attention, not for any personal qualities they possess or lack, but because of who they are by accident of birth. Once convinced that people stare because they are special, even the youngest twin may gain sufficient social poise to acknowledge this particular rudeness with a smile.

### What's in a name?

"I felt like a thing, not a person." When people stared at them, some twins felt that they were personally diminished, and for almost all of them being called "Twinnie" or "Twin" had had the same effect.

"I hated people calling me 'twin' instead of my name—after all they had a 50% chance of getting it right!"

"When our mother or father wanted one of us they would just shout 'Twin'. It didn't seem to matter which one of us replied."

"It didn't seem to matter" expresses the effect this habit has on an un-named child. In the survey, twins who had been treated in this way had come to believe that their dual identity was the only one that mattered.

"Because we were popular as 'the Twins'—I never thought anyone would want me as a friend for my own worth."

"We felt at times that people thought of us as one when we were together but only part of a whole when we were apart."

Several twins said they had this feeling of inadequacy, of not being a whole person, when their partner was not there.

To outsiders, it is easier to understand the working of this pair effect where identical twins are concerned but according to the survey this feeling is quite widespread. A fraternal girl remembered,

"Nobody ever recognised me as a real person—I always felt I was half of a twin, therefore I do not have any self-confidence or knowledge of what I really am like . . . My parents and school always treated us as equals and as a twin unit so I feel inferior now."

### Practical pressures

Not only did twins feel they were regarded and addressed as a unit they also encountered active opposition in their efforts to act independently and break out of this mould. In school, they met with resistance if they had wanted to study different subjects but most of all at home many twins felt under pressure not to rock the boat by being different.

"Parents, aunts and family expected you to do everything at the same time and in order not to disappoint you obliged until a point was reached when it became impossible."

"I hated the way everyone felt I should feel even though I didn't want to be a twin."

"Although I never consciously wished I wasn't a twin there were times it used to annoy me that we were clubbed together as The Twins—we were not often considered as individuals by the family group or by outsiders who knew our family."

This underlying attitude to twins in the family could now and then take a tangible form.

"At Christmas and birthdays when my grandmother gave us money to share—it was the same amount between us that she gave individually to all the other siblings."

"Because of our large family—twelve others, when it came to us there was never enough money to send us to music or dancing lessons, though each of the single sibs went."

"If there was something one of us wanted we were frequently told we couldn't have it because there were two of us to be considered. I realise that more often than not it could not be avoided especially when money was involved, eg school trips, but I remember feeling very resentful on these occasions because I wanted to know why we always seemed to be treated a little differently from everyone else."

Being unable to find twice the money for twins as for one child is firmly linked to undeniable hard facts. But the twins were not complaining so much at having to miss out as at not being treated the same as their other siblings. The solution may lie in doing just that. If, for example, twins can accept that it would be financially possible for both to go on a school trip if they were to agree to one going one year and the other the next, justice would be seen to be done even if they then decided for themselves that neither wished to go on their own. Parents are only likely to reach this judgement of Solomon however, if they themselves already think of their twins as being two separate and independent people.

*Being compared*

As the twins in the survey had resented being lumped together one might have thought that efforts to separate them out would have been welcomed. Unfortunately it is almost impossible to sort out one twin from another without comparing one with the other, and for twins, being subjected to these comparisons was a greater evil than the first.

Inanimate objects can be classified into simple groups like 'blues' and 'greens' but for human beings no comparison can be neutral. The comparison of two people inevitably presents one as somehow less good than the other, and by so doing detracts from what that one already has.

"The classic example was when I received 96% in a maths exam only to be asked what I had been doing because my sister had 100%."

Comparison is unpleasant for anyone, but for twins it touches an especially sensitive area as each may be privately using this method for himself to fill in the outline of his personal identity image.

"What makes me 'Me' is concerned with the areas where I differ from my twin," said one boy.

Resentment over a critical comparison with one's brother or sister may be compounded by guilt that one silently agrees with the comments being made.

Most twins had suffered from a comparison in class. Praise was difficult to enjoy because of the pain felt for the other's embarrassment.

"When my twin was hurt emotionally it hurt me as well. We both felt it would not have hurt if we had only been sisters."

The problem did not go away as their school life progressed.

"I felt I couldn't be outwardly pleased about my 'O' and 'A' level results because my twin did not do as well as I did."

And for some twins, comparisons were to remain a complication throughout life.

"There is always a feeling of guilt surrounding achievement in one's personal and professional life if the other one is not happy."

The one who comes off second best in comparisons may come to accept that view as true.

"Being constantly compared in looks, personality and intelligence—I only now realise how much it mattered."

Parents need to defend their children from this sort of thing, but sadly the survey showed that many of the most damaging comparisons had originated in the home.

"I will never forget being introduced to a visitor by my father as 'my son Ian's brother', when Ian was my twin."

The hard facts of life are however that there will be occasions when one twin will get more marks in exams, win more races, or just look more attractive.

"There have been times when I have been plainer than my sister and I hated the feeling that we were being compared and I was coming off second best."

Sometimes time will take care of such comparisons, but there will be some pairs where it is always going to be the same child who ends up feeling second best. Just as we tend to place two items close together in order to compare them better, comparisons are avoided if they can be placed far apart. Twins in this situation will benefit from attending different schools, and the effort to find two separate scout troops or a different hobby for each will be well worth the trouble.

## Being responsible for the other

"The only disadvantage of being a twin," said one girl, "is that you have two sets of feelings to hurt. A humiliation or hurt or even despair, affects the other equally."

Like the twin who said she felt her twin's embarrassment when they were compared in class, this twin spoke for many others in describing what had developed into a deep feeling of responsibility of one for the other. Several gave practical examples of what this had meant.

"Having to think about the other twin if you were asked out, I'd feel guilty leaving her at home. I felt that if I went out with a friend without her I was deceiving her. It is embarrassing if the other twin is not invited too—and upsetting if you are the one not invited."

Other close non-twin sisters may feel the same in some of the major events of their lives. A younger one who marries first, for example, may feel a twinge of concern that her sister may feel 'passed over'. Between twins, however, this sensitivity seems to be a fairly continuous state.

In the survey, where this concern for each other was mentioned, it was noticed that the younger they were, the more likely they were to include it in their comments.

"One disadvantage of being a twin is that I worry for my brother's safety all the time, and another is the pressure from working so we *both* do well at school . . ." said one eleven-year-old.

"My brother and I are close which means that we worry about each other as well as ourselves," said another schoolboy.

This feeling of joint responsibility goes even further.

"When she says and does things I don't like I feel partly to blame," said one girl.

Total involvement with each other's actions could have a stifling effect and some twins remembered the difficulty of breaking away.

"One disadvantage of being a twin was always having to take her feelings into account when I wanted something—it often ended up with a deliberate decision to be selfish."

Sometimes the kind of concern young twins had felt for each other seemed more appropriate to an adult role. When asked how he had felt when his brother had been rushed to hospital one identical twin gave the surprising reply:

"I was relieved because I knew that while he was there he could not be getting into trouble with the police."

Perhaps the normal sibling rivalry between spaced siblings serves the purpose of protecting children from carrying this sort of burden at too early an age. The boy of nine or ten who regards his brother's admission to hospital as a major drama to be enjoyed and retailed to his teacher may be showing a better emotional adjustment than the girl twin who cries hysterically every time her sister is bumped or scratched in the playground.

"See how well they look after each other!" is certainly a valid remark when twins hold hands going into nursery school, but should we not feel concern that a boy of fifteen is in a constant state of anxiety over his twin brother's possible delinquency? Parents of delinquent children feel such a worry is burden enough, and they can share it with each other. The twin who is bound to keep silent out of loyalty to his peers is doubly trapped and unable to discuss it when the subject of the trouble is his twin.

One of the interesting findings of this survey was that responsibility for each other was more frequently mentioned by male than by female twins. As boys are in general the least likely to invite discussion of their feelings it might be worthwhile for parents to assume that such a tie exists and allow their children some opportunity to express their concern for each other in a crisis. If this concern is not a feature of that pair's relationship no harm is done. One will soon know if one has made a wrong assumption.

"My younger son had to go into hospital when he was thirteen and his twin was about to go off to school without even speaking to him. I called him back and said, 'Aren't you going to say anything to John, he's going into hospital after all.' He came back and said—'Have a nice time!'"

## Parents 'pairing' again

A feeling of responsibility for one's twin did not appear to cloud one's sense of personal justice however. Several twins remembered with indignation what they had felt to be their parents' unfair treatment of them just because they were twins.

"My parents felt we were just as bad as each other so therefore we had to receive the same punishment!"

"I hated being a twin when I got told off just because my twin was."

Some parents were vaguely aware that to punish both might not be right but the alternative they chose seemed just as bad.

One of an identical pair remembered,

"When we were young and we did something wrong I used to get the blame as I am the eldest, even if it wasn't me, which I thought most unfair."

Treating one twin as the younger and the other as the elder came up repeatedly in other contexts too.

"I was not allowed to take the notes to school as she was the eldest."

This apportioning of blame and responsibility by difference in age is not only illogical where twins are concerned but dangerous for their development. The twin who is leader today will not necessarily be leader in six months' time. Twins tend to leapfrog each other in development so that to label one child in the pair as more capable can establish a straitjacket restriction on the potential development of both.

One adult identical twin told of the agonies she suffered having to screw up her courage to use the telephone on her first day at work in an office because as she explained, "Up to then my twin had always done that sort of thing."

## Becoming dependent

The danger of twins becoming cripplingly dependent on each other is often feared by outsiders, but it was interesting to find that this dependency was listed as a disadvantage by twins themselves.

Two elderly men writing from the same address said,

"The only disadvantage of being twins is that it makes you very dependent on each other which is a drawback in later life."

"Being inseparable and always having someone to go places with has made me lazy—I rarely do things alone," said another.

Boy/girl twins had also found this.

"Being a twin can be very restrictive, you tend to rely on each other's decisions, instead of making your own."

Twins tended to become dependent where the partnership had been working best. Many were able to comment on the result.

"Having a perfect companion has made me hypercritical of my friends and I find it difficult to communicate with other people."

Outside relationships measured by their twinship were almost always found wanting.

"We tended to have high expectations of people we met which we are only now beginning to lose," said one pair in their twenties. Used to their own effortless method of communication many twins found that similar relationships with others only came slowly. This proved disconcerting for some when the relationship was marriage.

At the early stages of development when twins get on well together it may seem pointless to think of separation, but once togetherness has become a habit there is no incentive for the twins themselves to try to operate apart. Parents too find it difficult to justify putting any pressure on a contented pair to act as individuals. In fact, one mother found it quite difficult to arrange.

"I found it needed special planning to get one twin on her own for any length of time . . . because they got on so well together. Recently one of them stayed with my mother for a few days and it benefited everybody. Both twins had individual attention and you get to know one on their own so much better. We plan to do it again."

The comment of one pair who had not had this opportunity would seem to confirm this parent's good sense.

"Being a twin was a disadvantage in that we did not become close to our parents as friends. We always had each other and left our parents out of our chatter—having seen my friends relate to their parents I feel I missed out somewhere."

*Disadvantage or not; should one interfere?*

When considering the disadvantages of twinship, some suggestions have been given as to how they might be avoided, but there is a school of thought which is sceptical of any interference.

"People think you should be treated specially which is rubbish. The more fuss made, the more you get the feeling you have three heads," said one identical twin who also has twins herself.

There is of course more than a grain of truth in this and so far as twin children are developing just like their other siblings this can be good advice. As the last example illustrates however, early recognition of potential disadvantages in twinship is not always easy. Our admiration for someone who says, "He's not heavy, he's my brother," should not however absolve us from giving him a hand with his load.

CHAPTER 13

# *Starting school*

Like other children twins will spend at least eleven years of their lives at school, and whereas the last chapters have given a general view of twinship, a look at the classroom can show us in more detail how a child may be affected by the fact that he is a twin.

## *The pair effect in the classroom*

Schools can be relied upon to react to twins in all the ways that are typical of society at large. The individual child is likely to be submerged within the pair, and parents may have to intervene to make him visible again.

"When I became a secretary in a college that my twin attended, I sneaked a look at his file, and was astounded to find a short résumé by his form master at his junior school, saying, 'Tom is a likeable boy, but totally overshadowed by his twin sister . . .' He then went on to list a couple of my shortcomings and lost sight of the fact that the report was on Tom."

School reports on twins should always be checked to make sure that what has been written does actually apply to the child to whom it belongs.

"When I left school certain teachers mixed up our reports. I ended up very poor in areas where I had excelled."

This does not only happen where twins are identical, as teachers like others seem to suffer a paralysis of their powers of recognition when they hear the word 'twin'. Being convinced that twins are difficult to tell apart, the majority do not even try.

Parents in the survey had sometimes been successful in helping teachers to separate their children in their minds by ensuring that, on open evenings, time was allocated for the dicussion of two children, and that they were not fobbed off with a catalogue of comparisons crammed into time normally allotted to parents of one.

Secondary schools had been found most likely to be guilty of lumping twins together. Teachers there tend to see pupils for shorter periods, and so take longer to get to know them individually. For twins this usually means an even longer delay before they are seen to be two people.

"Our teacher wondered why he had one of us, as he thought, for two lessons instead of one!" said one twin.

Unless it is pointed out to them, teachers in secondary schools will not expect to find two related children in the same year, a circumstance which another twin found to suit her quite well.

"I actually denied having a sister at all for six weeks after changing schools."

Infant and primary schools were much quicker to grasp the implications of twin relationships. Most parents agreed with the one who said,

"Infant and primary schools were very understanding, but the comprehensive, being a new idea, was oblivious to it all."

The mere fact that children are twins will tell a teacher nothing. What they need to know is how these children react within their twinship. Most parents who had discussed their twins with the school beforehand, found the teachers' subsequent handling of their children both sensitive and flexible.

"At five it was clear that Jean was brighter than Susan. Susan relied on Jean to do things for her and to talk for her. The classes were next door to each other and they were allowed to pop in and see each other whenever they wanted to. At first it was very frequent, but as they made their own friends, the need to see each other so often disappeared."

In other schools however parents found that the old blanket ideas about twins still lingered on.

"The headmistress had a policy of keeping twins together, and when they were nine years old, I had to struggle to get them to see that George was really suffering," said one mother.

Unless parents are alert, this old 'pair effect' will be allowed to overrule the children's own instinctive choice.

"On their first day at school our twins chose to be in different classes. Unfortunately, one of the teachers was a friend of the family, and decided that they should be in the same class."

Most twins do in fact start school in the same class. In the survey 97% of twins had started together. The majority of the remainder were in different classes because they were attending different schools. In eight cases this had been because one twin had to attend a special school for physically or mentally handicapped children. In one case the boy was being sent to an all boys preparatory school to escape the influence of his six sisters at home.

*Together or apart?*

This question does not have an easy answer. Even where a decision has been made in the interests of a specific pair of twins, circumstances in the school may hold one back. Not all teachers are as adept as others. Which twin should one send to the less popular teacher's class? Parents of identical twins also found that pupils could tell their children apart better where they had been kept together in the same class, as they had more chance to discover their distinguishing features. Separation is therefore not necessarily being advocated as a cure for all ills.

There are twins, however, who show signs that they would benefit from being apart long before the question of schooling has arisen.

"One of the mothers at our parents of twins club had one at nursery school and the other at home because she felt that one was ready and the other not . . . Knowing other mothers' experience gives one a bit of confidence to face people who may think you are cruel or even criminal to separate twins."

In some cases the signs in favour of separation may be quite clear.

"Just before he started nursery school John developed a stutter. Kenneth semed to be talking for him. If John started to say something, Kenneth would jump in first. After starting school in separate classes, John's stutter went, and he made a few friends of his own. But the funny thing was that the teacher discovered that Kenneth was more dependent on John, and not the other way round."

Quite often parents will have a 'hunch' about what is happening between their twins, and it is only when some action is taken that the underlying pattern of the relationship begins to show through.

One very clingy three-year-old surprised her mother by responding eagerly to the suggestion that she attend playgroup on one morning of the week without her socially more competent twin sister. Sure enough on arrival, she went off quite happily with none of the usual long parting scenes with her mother. The problem on previous occasions had been that she had felt unable to make an individual entrance while everyone's attention was focused on her more extrovert sister. The relationship between this pair had been one of rivalry since birth. In view of this successful experiment at playschool, separate classes seemed to be the best solution for this pair.

Not all children will give early indications of how their partnership is to develop. Some children will need much longer to explore the security of their dual role before they can benefit from the experience of independence. Five-year-olds who have already been apart at playgroup, or who have had frequent opportunities of visits to grandparents on their own, may be perfectly happy to settle in separate classrooms, but most head teachers would see parting from home and family as quite sufficient trauma for twins on their first day at school.

## But if not then—when?

In the survey 57% of twins who started school together were separated at a later date.

"At the age of eight we were put into separate classes—the head teacher thought it would be best—it lasted just two weeks. We got nothing done at all and were sick every night. These two weeks will stay with me for ever, and I will not let my own twins be deliberately separated for the sake of an experiment."

Eight is the age often suggested as being a good time for twins to be parted. Unfortunately however at this age they are regarded as being 'no longer babies', and what was appropriate for the five-year-old Susan and Joan may be regarded as childish nonsense to have to arrange for children of eight. Somewhere along the line close twins are supposed to have grown out of their interdependence, and its real effect on them is rarely understood.

"I remember when we were in infant school the teacher

wanted to move my sister to another table. This upset me so much that the teacher had to move her back. *I remember the fear of being without her.*"

If one is to help young twins discover that they *can* rely on themselves, one must accept that this fear is real. The same gradual approach that is applicable to the mastering of other fears is applicable here. Fear of the dark is not cured by forcing the child into a dark room, but by substituting a less and less bright light until the child can cope on his own.

Classwork naturally lends itself to short periods when twins may be split up unobtrusively, while yet remaining secure in the knowledge that when the job is done they can return to sit by their twin. They should for example certainly be in different groups for reading. Once they can cope with this they can be moved to neighbouring tables where they can still see their twin, and make eye contact. After that they can be moved even further apart. The first year at school should be used to introduce dependent twins to the discovery of their own feet, as this is just as much part of their education for life as learning to read and write.

It is significant that even twins who had been separated in infant school were more likely to become resigned to their lot when they could see some reason behind the move.

"I do remember we were always being told off for something, or teachers were frustrated and confused. We were only in infant school, five or six years old, when I remember this well-built lady taking us down the corridor one day, and sending us into separate classrooms, and saying to the teacher that we were not to be put into the same class again. I remember the feeling of disruption and confusion, but after that we were able to get on with our work."

Another twin had even clearer memories of why she and her sister were parted:

"I remember not concentrating so well when we were together—we used to look at each other and, thinking the same thing, giggle and more or less say 'it's your turn to put your hand up,' as the answer was always the same."

Another pair said quite simply:

"The reason we were split was that we used to get the giggles together."

Some twins in the survey not only accepted the reasons for their separation, but were surprised to find that they themselves preferred it that way.

"The teachers felt that we distracted each other too much, as we would fight for attention—I loved being in a separate class as I have a strong character and like being the centre of attention."

Twin girls, now teachers themselves, agree now from their own teaching experience that twins could distract the whole class by putting on a double act. They themselves recalled what they had felt at the time to have been an unjust warning letter sent only to their parents complaining of their behaviour, although the whole class had been involved.

"It was as though they thought we lay in bed each night planning the next day's mischief," said one, still indignant after fifteen years.

Her sister was able to remind her however:

"But that of course was exactly what we did!"

Naughty twins who were capable of getting amusement from their twinship rarely reported having found their separation at school to have been difficult.

"They used to squabble in class, even from opposite ends of the room—six months' separation in school soon put a stop to that," said one mother.

"We were separated because of academic ability. Later we were put together again, and our achievements plummeted, while our reputation for mischief soared."

Children are usually ready to accept a verdict if they are given a reason to support it, but it was amazing how many twins in the survey reported having been separated without any consultation or explanation.

"I don't know why we were separated, it was awful."

"We were put into different house groups much to our annoyance, as other siblings were not. We resented this, and expressed it either by protest or lack of co-operation."

There are in fact some very good and valid reasons why separation may suit some twins. There is also however an amorphous general impression among educators that separation, for twins, is somehow good in itself. Vague feelings about allowing twins to find their own individual identity are not sufficient justification for doing something which may appear to the children as a personal threat to their mode of life.

More worrying still was the lack of evidence of any schools having monitored the effects of separation on the pairs they parted. The twinship of the individual twin seemed to be quite forgotten once he was no longer seen as part of a pair. Parents at home, however, retaining their awareness of the children's twinship, could be usefully consulted as to whether parting them had been a good move.

"In the second year of senior school our twins were put into 'A' and 'B' streams by the school. We were not consulted or told why. Their class averages were only 1% apart. The result was that the one in the 'A' stream refused to work for his exams, as he wanted to be demoted."

The question of whether twins should stay together or not is best considered over a period of time, and not in response to the state of their relationship at one point only. Today's close dependence between one pair may well have changed to uninterest in six months' time. Unfortunately it tends to be the twins who are closest that teachers feel constrained to prise apart, while other pairs in the same class who are making all the effort they can to avoid each other, are seen to be managing their twinship very well, and in no need of separation. The dependent pair may however be turning to each other for support in reaction to current upsets at home; sudden separation in their case will only serve to increase their distress. A twin in another pair, trying desperately to get out from under his partner's shadow, would welcome the chance of escape into another class.

The tentative separation within the class was appropriate for twins in primary grades, but older twins who resist being parted need different handling. Clear explanations should help scotch the idea that they are being 'picked on' because they are twins, and a promise to review the situation after a set period of time might present the arrangement more on the level of a contract between equal parties, and less as an insensitive order from above.

There is no clear overall formula which can tell us whether any particular pair will benefit from separation or not. The formula 'try it and see' is probably best, provided that, (1) schools are willing to reunite twins if there is evidence that they are not being helped by being apart, (2) that parents feel strong enough to take up their children's cause with the school, and (3) that twins are honestly prepared to make a good case for whatever they feel best for themselves. 'No separation without consultation' would make a good banner for this cause.

We can however look at what did in fact happen to other twins in other schools. The twins in this survey were at school during the 1950s, when the general feeling tended to be that those born together should stay together. But even then more than half of them had been parted at one time or another.

*Separation Pattern of Twins in the Sample*

|  | SEP | Always Together |
|---|---|---|
| Identical Boys | 35% | 65% |
| Fraternal Boys | 60% | 40% |
| Boy/Girl Pairs | 67% | 33% |
| Identical Girls | 45% | 55% |
| Fraternal Girls | 80% | 20% |

*Reasons Given for Separation at School*

| Type of Twins | I boys | F boys | Boy/girl | I girls | F girls |
|---|---|---|---|---|---|
| School Policy | 40% | 5% | — | 40% | 28% |
| Teachers' Request | 36% | 5% | 14% | 14% | 3% |
| Parents' Request | – | – | – | 7% | 12% |
| Diff. 'O' and 'A' levels | 9% | 5% | 7% | 4% | 12% |
| Different sex schools | – | – | 27% | – | – |
| Too Dependent | – | – | 3% | – | 3% |
| Illness | – | – | 7% | 5% | 6% |
| Unequal Ability | 27% | 50% | 34% | 40% | 78% |

In some cases more than one reason was given for separation, or twins were separated on more than one occasion e.g. through illness in primary school and then again through choice of 'O' level subjects in secondary school. The above table does not therefore add up to 100 as would be expected.

It is significant that the most common reason for separating twins was not, as might have been suspected, the whim of the establishment, but related quite directly to the school's educational purpose being based on the academic ability of the children concerned. A breakdown of the other reasons which had been given for parting twins highlights some other interesting facts.

## School policy

When this was given by twins and their parents as the reason the children were separated, it usually meant that they had been given no reason at all.

"Their separation was a random action by the school—they were indifferent to it."

"School policy said separate classes at seven years old—they were shocked, but I am sure it was the best thing."

Parents who felt that their children had been parted merely as an experiment, and not from any knowledge of the relationship between their twins, exercised their right to remove their children from that school altogether. The twins' objections to separation by school policy was not always based on the removal of their twin's emotional support.

"We were annoyed," said one pair, "because it meant that we would have to work harder and do our own work."

It is highly suspicious that the spread of figures in the table shows that the twins most frequently separated on these grounds were the identical or visible twins. It could be that school policy was being applied to those who were seen to be twins, rather than to those whose twin relationship was seen as inhibiting their development. A teenage group of identical twins who by coincidence all attended the same school, were mildy resentful that they had all been separated as school policy. A set of fraternal boys in their year were still together they pointed out.

"And they hate each other and would give anything to be put into separate classes."

## Teachers' request

Teachers who requested that twins be separated did so from their personal knowledge of the children's development, and were quoted as having given reasons for their decision.

"It was suggested, if I did not have any objections, that the girls be put into different classes the following year, to ensure that the quiet one worked to her full capacity."

Another example illustrated how much staff were willing to put into finding out what was best for their pupils.

"They were slow learners and at primary school some teachers felt they were holding each other back. However, others disagreed, and they went back together after another year."

The mother in this case went on to say,

"Separation did them a lot of good socially but it made no difference to their academic progress."

So it is possible that both sets of teachers were right, but that some had a broader view of education than others.

The low number of fraternal girls who came into this category may reflect the high number who were entered as having been separated by 'unequal ability', which would have been another aspect of their teachers' having suggested separation.

### Parents' request

This category should also refer to the large number of parents in the survey whose request that their twins be separated was in fact refused.

"I had previously asked them to separate them at the age of seven years, as I felt neither was fulfilling their individual potential nor developing as separate people. This was refused, and I was treated like a 'stupid mother'. At eleven years, when it was quite wrong to part them as neither was ready or able to cope, I went as far as the County Education Office, but lost . . . The year they were apart did a lot of damage as they drew together even more and excluded everybody else . . . we eventually moved and they went to the same school again, but they were very immature compared to their friends of the same age."

This mother had other children in her family, so she was unlikely to have been blinkered in her views about her twins. Being treated as a 'stupid mother' by headmasters has been the lot of many parents of twins.

"The headmaster at their primary school told me that their education was his responsibility. They were happy and doing well and in his opinion nothing would be achieved by separating them. I tried again before they started secondary school, and they were treated individually. Both much preferred this, and I was happier."

Some parents only had a hunch that their twins might be better apart, but some had clear evidence that the school could not see them as individuals.

"I tried unsuccessfully to get them separated at nine years, but did not succeed until they were twelve. School reports were identical, and teachers could not tell them apart. At secondary school they were parted. They greeted this with relief, as they would no longer be compared."

Parents who were unsuccessful in getting schools to agree to separate their twins tended to be those whose children were identical pairs. Once again it was a question of the visible twins and society's reaction to them. One mother probably put her finger on it when she said,

"It was almost as though they were afraid to separate them."

Parents of boy/girl twins on the other hand were the most successful in persuading schools that their twins be separated, perhaps because of their being the least likely to be seen as a unit of two.

### Twins' request

This category does not appear on the table because it deals with those twins who would have liked to have been separated, but were never offered the chance. The girl of a boy/girl pair remembers:

"We were always in the same class even though I was not good enough for that grade. I hated school all the years I went. In primary school I was called lazy, and in secondary they said I did not try hard enough. No one knows how hard I tried except my twin . . . He used to tell Mum that I couldn't keep up in class, but I don't think she did anything about it."

Parents were quite often oblivious of how things were at school.

"The girl tells me now that the boy hated their being together in the same class, as she was top and he was bottom. They had their own friends and coped with their problem by ignoring each other at school."

*Different courses at 'O' and 'A' levels*

This category should be bracketed with the one above, as it is the twins themselves who make the choice of subjects they will study. Several twins in the survey gave this as a natural point where separation had seemed to them appropriate. Frequently they were apart for only one or two classes, but for those twins who have never been apart at all before their early teens, one class at a time is probably a good way to begin. One mother was able to see this gradual process of one class at a time bear some fruit.

"Over the last two years they have not been together for English, and I can now see their different views coming through."

Outsiders tend to forget that a separation from a lifelong companion in one's teens can be felt as keenly as it would have been at five years old.

"We were separated for 'A' level chemistry. Being in a different class from my twin for the first time I felt anxious, lost and a bit afraid."

This lad was fifteen at the time. Some late separations are obviously going to take a lot of sensitive handling.

As the fear that twin children will grow up too dependent on each other is the most commonly expressed concern of those dealing with twin children, it was interesting to find that this was seldom given as a reason for separating them in the survey. It is possible that some of those parted allegedly in obedience to school policy could just as well have been entered here.

The pairs who had been thought to have become too dependent on each other were not the identical pairs, but the boy/girl pairs and the fraternal girls. Once again we are reminded that the less visible twins are quite as likely to be affected by their life in tandem, and that this aspect of their development is often overlooked.


*Illness*

This was an interesting category, not so much as a reason for the separation of the twins, as for the opportunity it gave for the twins in question to comment on their feelings at the time.

"I was at school for a year without my sister. She was very ill in the last year of primary school. I think she missed me more than I missed her. I felt great being on my own. I suppose I had time to myself. I always liked to be with other friends, whereas my sister depended on me to look after her."

### Difference in ability

It comes as no surprise that among fraternal twins some were found to be cleverer than others. The high proportion of identical girls in this category was rather unexpected. So much attention is given to identical twins whose IQs are within a few points of each other, or who wrote identical essays word for word when working in different rooms, that we tend to lose sight of the fact that the likeness of many monozygotic twins is literally only skin deep.

Identical twins belong to a category in which some are more identical than others. But the twins themselves find it extremely difficult to convince outsiders of this fact.

"Our school deceived us into believing that our capacity was equal. I was quite pleased if someone noticed that I was the one who was more intelligent. I now feel that my twin is the successful one and I am second best. There is a lot of jealousy between us."

During the 1950s when these twins were at school, children were still streamed by ability so they could learn at their own rate. As this was not only happening to twins, but to their classmates too, one might have expected that separation on these grounds would have been easiest for twins and their parents to accept. In the event, however, the social and emotional implications of parting twins because of their unequal ability had distressed both twins and parents in the survey more than anything else.

# CHAPTER 14

# Coping with unequal ability

Parents of young twins often dread the inevitable day when one child will do better than the other. They may even be guilty of hoping that neither child wins a competition in order to avoid having to deal with the one who does *not* win the trip to Paris. Spontaneous praise for the winner of the race is sometimes held back for fear of damaging the self-esteem of the one who has not been placed. "This was the time I felt cut in half," wrote one mother.

The disappointed tears of a youngster who has lost a race can sometimes be dried by a quick reminder that although he lost here he won all the races at the Sunday School outing.

One mother said, "Fortunately, the one who didn't win had a loose tooth at the time so I was able to praise this up and take her mind off the race whilst at the same time praise her sister for winning."

It is worth burning the details of their past achievements into one's brain however, as it can be very difficult to summon up an equivalent achievement out of the blue just when it is required.

Chagrin at being the lesser is normally something these children will learn to cope with as part of growing up, but the survey showed that later on unequal examination results caused parents the same heartaches at an age where no loose tooth or past prowess could be called up in compensation.

The existence of a real intellectual gap between twins caused problems for many parents right from the start.

"The girl was a very early reader—at Ladybird six by the time she was four, whereas the boy was diagnosed as dyslexic and still (aged thirteen) receives remedial help with reading and writing. There have always been terrific problems educationally between them. You can't explain a twin's failure by saying, 'Well next year when you are the same age . . .'"

When the twins in the survey were at school every child sat a national examination called the eleven plus. On the results of this they were allocated either to senior secondary and grammar schools where the emphasis was on academic achievement, or to junior secondary and secondary modern schools where the pace was slower and geared more to the needs of the less scholastic child.

On the surface, this was a sensible arrangement. But by the time the twins in the survey were sitting it, it had acquired strong social overtones. It was far more prestigious to attend a grammar school than to go to a secondary modern and so the pressures on parents and children became enormous.

### Passing and failing the eleven plus

Although the system has now changed, there are still lessons to be learned from the ways in which schools, parents, and the twins themselves dealt with the fact that one twin had passed while the other had failed. The eleven plus may have gone but one twin may still be chosen for the team and the other not, one may be successful at an audition and the other not, and one twin may well come home with more 'O' and 'A' level passes than her twin.

The first mother said it all.

"This was the low point in bringing up the boys. There was still selection and although there had not seemed to be any great difference between them at school (if anything Trevor seemed quicker and good at general knowledge), it was Brian who passed the eleven plus. I was devastated and for the first time wept from sheer helplessness . . . I could only imagine the feelings of the twin who had been judged against his brother and found wanting—I tried so hard not to make too much of the successful twin's achievement that he said 'Aren't you pleased I am going to grammar school?'"

The twin who passed can also remember what he felt at the time.

"The teachers made us go into separate groups in the main hall and this really emphasised the split that was going to happen to us. The whole process was very arbitrary and I bitterly resented the fact that it made my brother so upset."

Another school was a little more sensitive in their handling of twins.

"At eleven years one of our twins failed the eleven plus. The headmaster discussed the matter with us and said we could insist that our boys be kept together and the Education Authority would allow the less academic one to stay with his brother. It was a hard decision to make but we had to look at the long-term effects and felt it would be a hard struggle for the less academic one to keep up with the amount of work involved. I am glad to say we chose the right line. The first two weeks were hard on both of them but they settled down and became 'individual' persons. The less academic one began to make decisions for himself and did well at school. He left at sixteen and served an engineering apprenticeship and is now going on to a staff position. Although a late developer he has done extremely well . . . Number two twin took 'A' levels and is now in his final year of a degree course in engineering."

It was interesting to notice that those twins who had been separated by exams at school very often ended up in the same job or profession. Two girls were even employed by the same bank, one getting there on her 'O' level passes and the other through evening class tuition.

Sometimes the difficulty of the decision was complicated for the parents by the fact that the school with the higher academic bent was fee paying, but by passing an entrance examination the child with ability who was less well off could win a free place.

"I feel our growing apart started when I was not allowed to take up the scholarship at the local high school. I can see my mother crying now but my father said one could not have something that the other couldn't have and as it was not possible to pay fees for my sister we would both go to the local secondary school, where I never had to work at all . . . My bitterness at my lack of qualifications stayed with me a long time . . . when my own children grew up I did some 'O' levels by correspondence . . . I have now been teaching for nine years and am doing an open university course."

One mother approached the problem from another angle.

"I was a bit upset when we sat our eleven plus. I passed and my brother failed. My mum said I should also re-sit it the following year then we could go up together."

Sometimes parents and schools saw the problem as insurmountable and so avoided it altogether.

"I was told I had failed my eleven plus and went to secondary modern school with my sister. Tracy couldn't spell so she had to attend a special spelling class once a week. My parents did not want us to be different so they made arrangements for me to attend too. I discovered last year that I *did* pass my eleven plus and before giving out the results they called my parents to the school and told them I had passed but my sister had failed. My parents' decision was to send us both to secondary modern stating that if I had the intelligence to pass the eleven plus it would not hinder me as I could attend technical school later on which I did—but I still feel very bitter about my parents' decision."

Only one of the families in the survey who had had to face this dilemma mentioned having asked their twins what they thought about the matter.

"The headmaster from their junior school came to see us and told us that only one of the girls had passed the eleven plus. He offered us a place at grammar school for both of them or a place at the comprehensive for both of them if we wanted. So we put it to the girls and said *if* one of you passed and the other didn't what would you like to do so they both chose to go to comprehensive school as it would be hard work for the one who didn't pass. There they did very well, both getting three 'O' levels and to this day we do not know which one passed and neither do the girls."

When children are brought into what they recognise to be a serious discussion their conclusions are not made on frivolous grounds as might be expected but on the same sensible grounds on which the adults would have based their decisions.

### The thoughts of the loser

Very few of the twins who had failed gave the impression of having carried any long-term personal scar from the experience of having been the least successful partner.

"I was disappointed that I did not pass the eleven plus but never resented my twin going up. I was pleased for her."

"At first I was devastated because the eleven plus was considered so important—but I didn't mind later on."

As was so often the case it was not the event but the comments made in connection with it that left the mark.

"I felt badly because she passed the exam. People used to say she was the clever one and I was the pretty one, I never got over that till I left secondary school and got my first job in a bank."

### Helping losers

If one is to compensate by comparison then one must get it right. Being "the pretty one" was no equivalent to being "the clever one" in the eyes of a twin who could later land herself a job in a bank.

Another parent was more successful in her choice of words.

"Mum used to say Dick had the brains but I had the common sense."

Helping children come to terms with their inequality of ability will often involve discussion with the one who feels aggrieved, but where possible the other twin should be included too as they will often contribute something which will help to even the score again.

"Although I had always realised Elizabeth was bright I didn't realise how bright. When she sat the eleven plus she gained top marks. Although she was granted an assisted place we've had to pay out a lot in fees, but felt at the time that we would regret it for ever if she were not given the chance. Jennifer said several times that Elizabeth was being "favouritized" to use her expression, and it was then that Elizabeth said she'd always felt deprived as a tiny child."

A family discussion may open up a Pandora's box of past problems but psychologists tell us that such things are better aired, and in this case everyone was given a second chance to redress the balance.

Treating one's children equally is often seen as the primary attribute of the good parent, but the blanket solution that salves the parents' conscience may not be right for twins.

"Because my twin was cleverer my parents put her in for the High School Entrance Exam. They put me in for it too, afterwards telling me rather clumsily that they did not expect me to pass, but they thought she might. I felt very hurt and would rather not have had the stress of the exam and wouldn't have minded her sitting it on her own. In fact she failed. We both passed the eleven plus. I remember there was a choice of schools and not minding where I went so long as we were separated."

As in almost every other case, discussion here might well have eased the situation for everyone.


## A parent's problem?

It is possible that coping with the apparently unfair unequal ability of twins is more of a problem for those of us who are parents than it is for the twins themselves. It was almost always the parents' mishandling of the situation that made the twins feel bitter and not their own adjustment to what was a fact of life. It was the parents in the survey who found 'trying to rejoice with one while at the same time commiserating with the other' 'an anguished struggle'. Still thinking about it even now that her children have grown up one still wrote, "I haven't found a good solution yet."

"Because of the lesser academic ability, my son was always less confident than my daughter, so we always tried to praise him for anything he did achieve and we encouraged him as much as we could. We did however criticise him if we felt it necessary but we always felt we needed to boost his ego."

This worked well for the less able twin although the mother was not so sure of its effect on the one who did well.

"We did praise her but not perhaps as much as we might have done had there not been the comparison with him . . . I know she has always felt guilty that she seemed to achieve more than he did with less effort and at one stage she said she wished she could give him some of her good results as he had to re-take an 'A' level. She was quite upset at the time."

Some parents managed to reassure the winner of their pride in his or her achievement by taking him or her into their confidence.

"Fortunately we had the kind of relationship where I could take the lucky one aside and say, 'Look, you have done absolutely marvellously and we are thrilled to bits but I know you will understand if we play it down a bit won't you?' They always understood."

One mother who had had to deal with the situation more than once suggested,

"Perhaps we should not let them do everything together from birth—let them have a special thing of their own and encourage the other in something else—I think I could have helped them earlier than school days to get used to the idea that they would be good at different things."

*Will all twins be upset?*

The amazingly simple answer to this is, "Ask them and see."

"I was moved up a class in the fourth year. I later discovered that the teachers had been debating for a long time whether it might not be harmful to split us up and that my exam results were such that I really ought to have been moved up into a higher class a whole year earlier than I was! Neither of us were consulted (at fifteen or sixteen years old!) as to whether we would object . . . Once we were apart my sister's work improved and I went into Class 'A' . . . now I think they should have done it earlier."

One twin who was consulted by a wise headmistress wondered what all the fuss was about.

"At age seven or eight it was proposed that my twin brother miss the first class of junior school because he was so clever. I remember being taken to the headmistress who wondered if I minded about this—I didn't mind at all. After this we were never in the same class again. He went to grammar school and I went to secondary modern—I was much better at sport."

Given an early chance to get used to their differences many twins like the one above found their own compensation by excelling in another field of their own choice.

When the difference in ability matters to the twins they themselves will react.

"My parents were super but they did not realise what was happening in school and why I was rebelling so . . . When my sister was cleverer I retaliated by being better at getting into trouble . . . At my request we were in separate classes for our last year at school and my work improved."

When things are not going smoothly between twins, parents should not shy away from the possibility that the underlying cause may be that one is brighter than the other. It is a situation which can be alleviated by reducing the amount of time during which they can be compared.

Having lived with each other all their lives, twins know better than anyone about the differences that exist between them and many will welcome a chance to escape from the comparisons that they themselves are forced to acknowledge by forced proximity.

One twin remembered,

"I passed my eleven plus and my sister didn't—we were sent to separate schools. I was glad to be free from competition, and free from pressure from my twin . . . I felt gladly individual."

# CHAPTER 15

# The pressures of proximity

Just over 50% of the twins in this survey had been separated at school. That leaves just under 50% who spent the whole of their school life together. A look at how individual twins coped with this constant close proximity in the classroom may give us some idea of the type of adjustments they have to make in other spheres to preserve the equilibrium of their life as a pair.

What goes on between the two who make up a pair is not what goes on between them and the outside world.

"If for example we were competing against each other, say in sport or indoor games, we would usually try to beat each other. But if a third party or parties were involved it did not really matter which one of us won, we'd work together to make sure that one of us did."

This twin reaction to competition with outsiders is harmless enough in sport but in the classroom setting it can be strong enough to interfere with the learning process.

"When I could answer a question in class that my sister couldn't we experienced a sort of panic and a great desire to answer for each other . . . We always tried to do our best in order not to let the other down. I felt hurt if my sister was given less marks than me. I could never start an exam till I saw my sister had actually started to write as I was not at ease until she had done so. I am the oldest by three minutes and felt a responsibility towards her that I could not let her down by starting when she couldn't."

Sometimes it was only the absence of the other twin which brought to light just how much this shouldering of responsibility for "the other" had become a part of life.

"When we went to separate schools I was glad to be free of the worry of how my twin was getting on." In the survey those twins whose relationships were bound by such close emotional ties were in the minority but even those with less obvious emotional bonds also made adjustments to suit their life within the pair.

As we saw in the last chapter, twins in the same situation may well react differently. What is pleasant for one can be hurtful to the other's self-esteem. Where this is the case, adjustments are made much as the oyster smoothes the satin surface of pearl round an irritating piece of grit, for the mutual comfort of the pair.

### How twins adjust

Many twins found that they rationalised differences which existed between them to reduce disappointment and minimise embarrassment.

"I was overall cleverer . . . We put my slight edge down to her bad handwriting since she was left-handed."

"I accepted the fact that I was slower to read because I had had ten weeks in hospital."

The most common self-justification used by the cleverer twin to ease his mild guilt at being better at things was, "Well, after all I am the elder by five minutes!"

Where one could not neutralise comparisons with some sort of reason—they hurt.

"When I was the cleverer I felt guilty as it made the other twin feel upset—this took away all the pleasure of doing better."

### Working as one

Different twins in the survey coped with comparison in different ways but definite patterns did emerge. It would be too simplistic to say that where there was a difference in ability the clever one held back, or that the slower one allowed the bright one to do the work for both. The variations were much more subtle.

"I never felt we were competing, we were as one, not two individuals," said one pair.

Where the brighter child seemed to do all the answering, it did not necessarily mean that the other twin was being lazy. Quite a few of the younger children saw themselves operating as a pair and not as individuals at all.

"In junior school when a question was asked Stuart's hand

always shot up and I think Peter thought, 'Well, we've answered that question now'. At seven it was difficult for them to understand that working together was seen as cheating."

Twins themselves remember their thoughts:

"When my twin did better than me it made me feel proud of her and also I felt I needn't make the effort—the reflected glory was enough."

"It never occurred to me to compete as such. I think it was more a case of capitalising on her superior knowledge—especially where homework was concerned."

In some cases however the brighter child began to find that too much dependence had become a burden.

"My sister never wanted to work in school. I preferred to be in a separate class because Jenny was always copying my work and I was having to help her."

*Competing to be the same*

Some children who had begun to feel the strain of the gap between their abilities made another adjustment which was for both to try to be the same.

"We both had the same IQ but I must admit that if I said I did not remember a certain thing and we were having a test we both got it wrong on purpose. My parents never found out until we were laughing about it years later."

One mother noticed this happen:

"Shula is the brighter one of the two but I feel she applies herself to the utmost only when Angela's performance is comparable with her own, and if Angela is falling back then she lets up too. Maybe it is my influence as I make them expect to do as well as the other."

In the survey this turned out to be the most common way for twins to adjust so that it is unlikely that this mother's attitude had made much difference in this case. Another parent had also noticed it happening in infant school.

"They encouraged each other with their work but liked to be at the same level in sums and reading. I feel they held back for each other."

Where keeping level was important to a pair of twins they found ways of ensuring that that was what happened.

"Generally we were the same but if not we copied each other's work."

There is something here that is different from the copying of the single child who has forgotten to do his homework and hopes to get by by subterfuge. A twin's urge to copy may need to be dealt with in terms of the relationship with his twin rather than in the straightforward context of cheating.

### Who benefits?

Competing to be the same can mean that the brighter child is holding back, which can be worrying, but it may also mean that the less able child is being stretched to make more effort and so be forced to achieve more than he or she would otherwise have done.

"Up to moving to junior school the boys proved to be above average with school work, but when they separated it seemed that the younger twin had no guideline—like how hard to work. The older one carried on working well but the other one began to drop behind in his work and his reports were not good."

Other parents had found the same thing.

"They said the first twin was doing better than the second one and suggested that they be separated. They were about level when they went into different classes. They reacted badly. The first twin did not do any better and the second just went downhill."

Re-uniting a pair like this may be worth trying, as keeping level together can have a positive effect as each child aims at a sensible goal. In theory the goal of every pupil should be to achieve 100%. As this is unlikely to be within the reach of most however some more acceptable standard tacitly agreed between twins can effectively inspire more effort from the one who has to work harder.

Parents had seen this at work.

"He was much cleverer at first as he learned more easily—our daughter seemed stupid when young, this made her work hard fortunately and she achieved more 'A' levels than the boy."

Even the twins remembered this taking effect.

"My twin was cleverer than me and I suppose I used to try and keep up with her. Looking back I think I might have been lazier if I hadn't had that pressure to keep up."

This mechanism also worked for pairs who were competing to outdo each other as well.

"It was always more important that I had beaten my twin in class not that I had beaten my classmates."

And another pair wanted to remain together for just this reason.

"They did not like being separated because they could not compete with each other."

Using each other's results as a guideline caused a different problem for those twins whose ability was almost equal.

"The biggest problem at secondary school was the fact that each measured herself against the other. Although there was no aggression involved in this, it meant if one received a lower grade than the other she regarded herself as a failure."

"If my twin overtook me I had a massive inferiority complex because although she was only slightly better at school work she'd come top and I'd be second."

One pair of identical girls preparing for their 'A' levels told how they would listen on first waking to hear if the other was already up and if so would leap out of bed to catch up in case the other had managed to complete more revision by being up first. Spurring each other on to higher and higher grades was most often reported by the identical girls in the survey but some boy/girl pairs had also operated in this way. When their attitude was, "If she could do it then so could I," this system worked well but they tended to denigrate their own ability unjustifiably when even a slight gap opened up between them, and so developed an unrealistic image of themselves.

## Avoiding the issue

Children of equal potential did not always produce equivalent results. Where the difference between them mattered to them, they had dealt with it in one of two ways. By the first they preserved the less able twin from constant disappointment and by the second the brightest twin consciously provided an area where the other twin might shine.

*Refusing to compete*

"The quicker twin seemed to have a leaning towards music, playing certain pieces by ear on the organ so I took them both to lessons. The teacher said in front of them, 'This one is far quicker isn't she?' The other immediately said, 'I am left-handed,' and refused to go again although she sometimes has a go at home."

Another twin had taken the same way out saying,

"There was no point in working if you were always going to be compared with your twin."

There was evidence of this happening even where twins were of similar ability.

"I obtained slightly better marks in physics two years running so that my sister was not top of the year. Strangely she lost interest in the subject which may have been due to this."

This reaction can also confuse the issue in primary schools where children have just begun to learn.

"Both we and the school knew that Peter was the cleverer but he seemed not to try and just daydream. We realised this when Helen was off school with jaundice and Peter came home pleased that day and said, 'Good, I will be able to catch up on her reading books,' but that afternoon he came down with jaundice so missed the opportunity of being at school on his own. On their return he just seemed to lose interest. The headmaster agreed to put him in another class of a similar grade and in the end they both ended up taking six 'O' levels so there was no difference between their intelligence. In the beginning he must have felt there was no point in working because he was so much in her shadow."

The twin relationship affected children's willingness to make an effort in other areas too.

"Because Stephen's slight cerebral palsy limits him in all things sporting, we felt that Tony never tried and are relieved that he seems at last to be enjoying his bicycle."

*Allocating territories*

Twins were quite specific about this second way of avoiding painful comparisons.

"If one of us was good at a subject there was no point in competing. We 'divided' the subjects we were good at—me for art and her for maths and so on. We never consciously competed with each other . . . Perhaps we were unconsciously afraid of upsetting the balance."

"Mary was better academically but also liked art but art was Elizabeth's best subject so Mary did not pursue it."

Some twins described their division of interests as a fortunate circumstance but as it was a very common pattern among the twins in the survey it is much more likely to have developed out of a very early conscious choice to avoid being in competition.

"I think we were both fortunate to excel in different areas. I was more academic than my brother, he was practical and athletic. We were never rivals in anything but we always enjoyed it if the other won something."

"When I did well in class and beat my sister I always knew she was better at other things. I never felt I was competing so I didn't worry."

*Individual praise—a rare experience for twins*

Every parent hopes that their children will find their own area in which to shine whether they are twins or not. Where twins had done so parents in the survey, not surprisingly, reported jealousy to be at a minimum and that each had praised the other when they did well.

It is however much easier to encourage different interests in children of different ages. Twins will tend to want to join the judo class together, or to enrol for brownies at the same time. Because they are the same age it seems the obvious thing for them to do. Parents who had tried to encourage their twins to diversify had found it difficult to persuade the children to agree. But two families had worked out a way.

"We would allow them both to join things like dancing or gymnastics but as soon as one lost interest we allowed her to leave while the other continued, whereas with a single child we might have insisted that she stick with her original choice at least till the end of the term."

"Murray came home from school one day crying 'Angus is cleverer than me.' We had always known this of course but had taken care to emphasise that they were both clever in different ways. Angus 'had to be best' but Murray was physically more advanced and could be encouraged to take up sporting rather than academic activities. We bought each child—that is all three of our children and not just the twins—a small plaque on which could be stuck various badges for different achievements. The badges were often different on each plaque but the total ended up the same."

The old 'pair effect' very often inhibits parents of twins from encouraging only one of the partners to take up an interest. Having called one of our children to look at the foreign stamp which has arrived in the post we are suddenly guilty that we called this one and not the other. We are of course responding to a subconscious awareness of real differences between them. Even at an early age when no particular bent is obvious, parents pick up indications of how their children's personalities are going to develop. The mother in the music hall joke who said she thought her son was destined to be a surgeon from the careful way he cut up his meat may not have been so very far from the mark!

A butterfly once settled on our kitchen window and without thinking I found I had called only one of my daughters to come and see it. They were only toddlers at the time and I was puzzled as to why I had not called them both. Seven years later, seeing that child bent in concentration over an exquisitely detailed drawing, I know why it was she who had come to mind at that moment. Perhaps this is what the mother in the previous chapter meant when she said she felt that she should have encouraged her children to understand that they would be good at different things when they were very young.

From the adjustments that we have seen the twins in this chapter make at school, it is clear that there are mechanisms within their twin relationship which can allow individual differences to emerge. It is therefore up to parents and teachers to work along with this and not to constrict the development of individuality within partnerships by treating all twins as a pair.

# CHAPTER 16

# Role taking and role giving

It became clear from the survey that adjustments in class were only one aspect of the general pattern of adaptation which twins develop in order to ease the pressure of life as a pair. Some safeguards had quite consciously been worked out.

"We were very careful about hurting each other's feelings as children and devised codes that could avoid this. For example, we decided that I liked the colour blue, and she red, so that if we were given two of anything and they were coloured we could choose without fear of taking the one the other wanted. We were perfectly aware that often it was the shade that counted—a perfectly vile pink just didn't balance with a nice blue—but we had to stick to the code so we were sure of not hurting each other."

More often, however, the balance within the relationship had been achieved by less obvious means.

"It was the temperament that made the difference," said one mother.

Some pairs appeared to polarise into one extrovert, one introvert, or one leader and one led. The father who had provided his family with the achievement badges had found one of his twins to be more competitive than the other saying,

"He always had to be first."

Another father described his second twin as having "An almost desperate determination to win. It was as though having been held up by the other at birth he had decided never to let anyone obstruct his path again."

### The dominant twin

Parents are often apprehensive that the more assertive child will ride rough shod over the quieter partner but the survey showed that in many cases these appearances of strength could be deceptive.

When apparently dominant-dependent pairs were separated at school, the previously competent child was often the one who took longer to settle to his new situation.

"In outsiders' eyes the 'leader' was the elder twin who appeared much more confident and outgoing. On their first real separation my own feelings were confirmed as the 'leader' went completely to pieces and could not cope. She needed the quiet strength which seems to come from the younger twin."

In some cases, one can see a pattern being laid down almost as soon as the twins can toddle.

"During the day my mother-in-law sat watching the children and noticed the same thing being repeated several times. Karen would find a toy to play with and Debbie would immediately take it from her. Karen did not object and seemed quite happy to let her have it. She would then choose another. Debbie would then take that too. By the end of the afternoon Karen had changed her behaviour. When Debbie took the first toy she would then go immediately to the box and get another so that when Debbie, as expected, took that too she was able to repossess the first toy and carry on playing where she had left off."

The child who seemed to have been bullied by her sister had made a very mature adjustment. By the age of twenty months, Karen had already begun to organise her own behaviour to allow for the quirks in her sister's personality. The quieter twin of a pair may have had the most experience of having her wishes obstructed but because she has also made all the adjustments for the smoother running of the partnership, the 'bossy' one has not had the same opportunity of learning how to deal with frustrations.

This underlying pattern will often persist without the knowledge of teachers or parents.

"I was the dominant personality when we were children. Our mother would tell me to ask at the shop when we had an errand to run: by the time we arrived there I had always persuaded my sister to ask instead."

The apparently stronger and more dominant child may be the least able to take the responsibility she is given and if she is not able to off-load it on to her twin, being constantly seen in this role may become a strain later in life.

"We both left home when we were seventeen and moved to London. Although outwardly I was the more successful twin I found it more difficult to cope and at the age of twenty had a nervous breakdown."

## The quieter twin

"They rarely quarrel because Avril always lets Lucy have her own way," said one mother, and another describing the same sort of relationship between her twins said,

"Sarah never thought winning worth the fight."

Although the Avrils and Sarahs of this world contribute greatly to the peace of family life they do have a tendency to transfer this piece of social learning to the other fights outside their twinship. This is often the twin who will avoid competitive games but on a more serious level her performance in class may be affected by this otherwise sensible attitude of resignation.

A teacher, herself a twin, and the mother of twins once observed,

"I have done a lot of remedial work in the last twenty years and I have frequently had to cope with one twin being well behind the other in school work. Motivation was always difficult with these children because they were invariably the better natured of the twins and quite willing to accept the 'thick' label put on them by their peers."

## The dependent twin

Not all partners of assertive twins will be accepting and quietly strong. Some *will* be waiting until their twin has tired of the limelight so that they too may have a chance to shine but there are others who seem ready to surrender their right to any light at all.

"If my sister did not like my boyfriends I gave them up . . . I thought I didn't need friends as she was always there to help and advise. Now in my twenties I find it very hard to make friends and keep them. My parents did try to warn me saying she would not always be there but I found it hard to accept."

Dominant twins will sometimes acknowledge that having had

to support a dependent partner has helped improve their own image of themselves.

"She is twenty minutes younger than me—I feel protective towards her and I like that feeling," said one nineteen-year-old. Perhaps parents could learn from this and apply the same technique to help enhance the self-image of their less confident child. A dependent twin's self-esteem can also be improved if he can find someone else outside the partnership who will rely on him in the same way he relies on his twin. Some children manage to arrange this for themselves.

"One of our twins seeks out lesser mortals with problems, ie new children at school to look after, it makes him feel useful."

These are sometimes the children who will choose younger children to play with and they should be encouraged in this. Some of us need to retrace our steps to the last level at which we felt confident in order to re-secure a better foothold from which to make the next move up. Playing with less threatening children not only allows a dependent twin respite from 'having to keep up' but will also increase his opportunity to experience some time on his own. Temporary partings for this pair may indirectly also help the stronger twin.

"I would meet my friends to get away and be on my own," wrote one twin, "but this was difficult as she would always want to come with us."

"I felt quite independent," wrote another, "but my twin would not go anywhere without me. If I was sick she would stay off school as well."

Intervention is needed here to ensure that the dependent twin does begin to find her own feet, but it is also needed on behalf of the stronger child so that she does not begin to find her twin a burden.

Parents will quite often persuade twins to go out together on the grounds that there is safety in numbers but a little thought will show that each child out separately with another friend also meets this requirement.

Twins can be taught very early that each is expected to take responsibility for himself. Children who take dinner money to school, for example, should each take their own even if they are in the same class. On the day no change can be found and it has to be sent in a lump sum, asking one twin whether he minds that the

other takes it is probably sufficient to let him know that each one
is seen to be equally capable of the responsibility.

## Leapfrogging

Although by adulthood twins may have settled into roles which
can be clearly described, arriving at a comfortable balance within
the partnership is not done overnight. Parents of twins are often
disconcerted when their 'more mature' twin seems to regress and
for no apparent reason their shy one steps out of his shell.

From infancy it is well known that the physical development
of even identical twin children appears to develop by a leapfrog
process. One will learn to walk first but a month or two later it
will be the other one who is the first to speak. Temperamentally
too, last month's "Goodie" tends to become this month's
"pest", just like the two little bears in A. A. Milne's poem.
"Their personalities were always changing—weekly, monthly,
six monthly and eventually yearly . . . when one was domesti-
cated and helpful the other was tomboyish and defiant. As the
intervals of change became longer it was more difficult to
appreciate that."

## Changing roles

The smooth running of a partnership where both play their
accepted roles can be disrupted if some outside influence induces
this sort of change.

"The quiet one accepted being dominated until the age of four
when she had her tonsils out after which she became bigger and
stronger and for the first time hit back—the other twin was very
alarmed about this, shouting, 'Mummy, Mummy she hit me
back!'"

Some situations are quickly resolved but in others time may
elapse before it becomes clear quite what is going on.

"During their second year at school the quiet one was
fortunate in having a very understanding teacher who we think
improved her self-confidence. The puzzling thing was that her
behaviour at home became unbearable. Near the end of this
phase I heard her order her usually dominant sister to fetch the
paint box and waited for the angry refusal. None came. Then I

realised what all the trauma had been about, they had reversed roles. Had I not been concentrating on trying to cope with the first child's bad behaviour I might have cottoned on sooner as her sister had also been moving her stance from being bossy to being quite clingy and even at eight years of age, suddenly wanting to sit on my lap."

*Labelling*

In the normal course of events twin children will arrive at those complementary roles which are comfortable for them within their pairing. That does not mean to say that they will stay that way for ever. The couple effect means that a change in one will tend to be followed by a complementary change in the other so that a balance can be maintained. We should expect twin children to change as they develop and grow. Problems will arise for both children if we label them for life.

All parents put labels on their children. "And this is the baby" we say fatuously as we introduce a six foot seventeen-year-old son. Everyone can see in this instance that the label does not apply but in the case of twins labels tend to be seized upon as a means of identity and because they may serve this practical purpose they are likely to stick.

"I think it was my fault that Sheila was the leader. She was the first born and smallest and when I brought her home from hospital they told me to feed her and see to her first, and unfortunately I carried on putting her first, right up to school age. The best thing that happened was that they decided to go to different universities. Once away from Sheila Katherine came out of her shell—if anyone had said to me in her last year at school she would have been able to stand up in court and speak to a judge, I would not have believed it, she was so quiet and shy."

Slipping twins into special roles is so easy that parents do not know that they are doing it. Even those who might have been expected to have been on their guard have been caught out.

"I took the boys with me one morning to the canteen of the clinic where I work as a child psychologist. A colleague who had seen us there asked me, 'Do you always listen to what the little one has to say before you give the big one a chance?' I was shocked because when I thought about it, I saw that he was right."

## Labels

The problem with labels is that they stick even when they have been outgrown and have a restrictive effect on individual development.

"From my parents' description and stories when we were young, they certainly called my sister the more demanding one. I was the passive one—but I guess far more anger was in me but I didn't show it—I tried to get the attention by being 'good'. Your passive one may not be so passive internally."

Even more dangerous is the labelling which does not attach to the individual child but rather to the twinship itself. Some parents could only cope with their pair by seeing them as one good twin and one bad twin at all times. A teenage boy qualified his remark, having asked his father for something on behalf of his twin with the explanation, "It was his turn to be out of favour that week." He regarded this as one of the harmless inconsistencies one had to put up with from parents. But twin girls who spoke of this felt there was much more to it in their case.

"My twin and I resented, and still do, being played off one against the other by our mother. My mother can't have us on good terms with her at the same time . . . This treatment . . . has brought my twin and me closer together."

If parents suspect that they might be doing this subconsciously it might be worth bringing it out into the open. Asking the twins, "How is it I can't seem to have you two both in my good books at the same time?" could clear the air and bring some answers for all concerned.

## The permanent black sheep

But sometimes our disapproval does not fluctuate between the children but remains firmly centred on one child alone. There can be few parents who have not found themselves caught up at some time in an unreasonable cycle of irritation towards one of their offspring. And it is so much worse when the 'bad' child is one of a pair.

The dynamics here are the same as those in a matrimonial quarrel. Every move the child makes seems designed to annoy. The child feels the hostility and makes some kind of reply which then justifies our annoyance and the reaction is circular. Something is needed to jerk the needle out of the groove in the record so that harmony can be restored. Parents tend to describe these times by saying "He is going through a terrible phase", but it is just as likely that it is the parent who is going through the phase. There are many reasons why parents may "take against" their children, but some of those are to do with the roles that we have put upon them.

"Right from birth Sarah had been the good child in every possible way, whereas Stephen had been much more difficult. He was an extremely clumsy child (he is left-handed which had always caused difficulties), and however hard we tried not to, we always seemed to be at him. Consequently as the years went by if there was any trouble we automatically assumed it was Stephen's fault. This has had two results, first that he has become somewhat defensive and occasionally deceitful, secondly Sarah, I am sure, feels she has to become extra good 'for' him—and also feels responsible when he is in trouble for something. Now that I am aware of the problem I am trying to do something about it—and it is not as bad as it was . . . I feel very guilty at having made Sarah feel responsible and guilty herself—but hopefully things won't get any worse."

### The pain of preference

The most difficult situation arises when we ourselves have a conscious preference for one child. One could write a whole book on that subject and Marion West has. In *Two of Everything but Me* she tells of her struggles against her preference for one of her twins.

"One day when they were about three, Jeremy climbed a tree. Jon followed looking scared. He begged 'let's get down brother'. Jeremy refused and Jon stayed in the tree but he looked miserable. I was angry but I couldn't say—'I'm angry with you because you don't like to climb trees.'"

One of the mothers in the survey remembered how she had been helped with a similar problem.

"I needed a psychologist to sort me out over this. J. and I were heading for a breakdown in relationships at about the age of eight years. The psychologist was fantastic. He said, 'You are the adult and you will have to change.' I did—I had to pretend to love him and he responded and then I began to love him and now I adore him. He is still my ugly duckling but we love each other deeply."

Every parent in the survey who talked of having been caught in the trap of seeing one twin as exclusively good and the other as exclusively bad, commented on how the struggle through this bad patch had allowed this child to share something extra with them in the end. Once the problem had been resolved it is also nice to know that it is unlikely to remain in the memory of the child as anything more than, "Oh you mean that time when we went to that doctor and you cried?"

## Finding the balance

Happily not all twins will polarise into good, bad, dominant, dependent, or leader and led. Some will exchange these roles off and on over the years and others will seem to be level pegging all the way.

"Twin one was usually the leader but the support and approval of twin two was always important to him and he was quite prepared to modify and alter his plans if his suggestions were not approved by his twin."

The twins in the survey sorted out the roles within their pairing as they progressed through primary school. By the beginning of their secondary education, many had achieved a comfortable balance and had worked out a mutual strategy of dealing with pressures from outside. But what neither they, nor their parents, had expected was that at adolescence new pressures arising from within their partnership might upset this hard won balance once again.

# CHAPTER 17

# Extrasensory perception

The separation of twins is an idea which tends to arouse a feeling of faint unease. What if the quality of their closeness were based on more than a mutual accommodation to their parallel development, and what if it extended beyond a conscious concern for each other into the region of an extrasensory perception? Might not any move to disturb their relationship be tampering with a Pandora's Box better left strictly alone?

Telepathy and extrasensory perception have been the theme of countless fictional tales about twins. Actual reported cases are always welcomed as good copy by the media. The fact that apparently authentic incidents baffle science only adds to their popular interest and most of us would feel let down if it were ever proved that this uncanny communication between twins had a mundane explanation. The supernatural overtones of the subject lead to a rather confused misapplication of the injunction, "What God has joined let no man put asunder" when the question of separating twin pairs is brought up.

*How can one connect experience of ESP with the quality of twinship?*

As with other aspects of the paranormal, it has proved virtually impossible to set up any controlled scientific experiments which will pin-point the nature of any special form of communication between twins. The Birmingham Family Study have done a recent study where paired subjects were put into different rooms. One was then asked to draw a square, circle or triangle and the other asked to predict which it would be. The results failed to show twins to be any better at guessing what their partner might do than unrelated pairs who had also taken part in the project. Studies like these can prove that this is not the sort of extrasensory perception which twins experience. They do not disprove that they feel anything at all.

Unfortunately of course all such experiences tend to be reported by those to whom they have happened. Unbiased witnesses are extremely difficult to find and almost all accounts are likely to be dismissed by scientists as anecdotal or founded on hearsay. The survey undertaken for this book was by definition based on the personal, subjective accounts of twins and their parents, and so as such they cannot pretend either to prove or disprove the existence of extrasensory powers. What they did do however was to show up a pattern among the types of experience reported and the sorts of circumstances in which they were most often said to have been observed.

The question for both parents and twins was,

"Have you or your twin(s) had any experience which might be explained as being able to read each others minds? If so, what?"

The twins were also asked,

"Have you ever been surprised by both of you having the same illness or pain at the same time?"

Out of the 600 participants who filled in questionnaires, 183 claimed to have had some experience of this sort which appeared to be directly tied up with the fact that they were twins. There were others who had had experiences which they felt might qualify but which at the same time they felt would be equally well explained by the workings of coincidence.

Several said quite firmly,

"We had a close relationship and often knew what the other was thinking—but it was not ESP."

Others said, "I don't think I would know where shared experience stopped and ESP began."

*Society expects twins to experience ESP*

183 people in the survey claiming to have experienced ESP leaves 417 twins or parents of twins who made no such claim. The majority of twins do not in fact claim to be able to communicate with each other in any special way but several of those in the survey felt that they were under considerable pressure to do so.

"Sometimes I lie there thinking, am I getting a message or is it indigestion?"

"The only time it ever bothered me," remembered one boy, "was when my sister had her first baby. I was on night shift and couldn't really settle to my work for fear of getting her labour pains."

Some twins felt annoyed when outsiders asked if they had ever experienced any supernatural communication with their twin.

"I feel people are being personal . . . and trying to find out about something they cannot hope to feel."

Twins who objected on these grounds suspected the questioner of scepticism but others felt such enquiries to be quite normal and only felt sorry that they were unable to keep the conversation topic going with anecdotes of their personal experience.

### Is ESP dependent on a close relationship?

Twins are not the only people to claim special powers of communication. The late Travers Christmas Humphreys, one of England's high court judges, claimed to be able to contact his wife by telepathy, which he remarks in his biography could be very useful on occasions when he had to let her know that he had been held up in court. In their case as husband and wife, one tends to assume that this sensitivity must be based on sympathetic involvement with the other person concerned.

To test this idea a comparison was made between twenty of the identical girls in the survey who had claimed to have experienced ESP and who had also at some point in their questionnaire made reference to the type of relationship they had enjoyed with their twin.

9 were happy close pairs
6 regarded themselves as not very close
3 were often in disagreement and had had a stormy partnership since childhood
2 were resentful of their twinship and as adults had little to do with each other

According to this group therefore sensitivity to ESP would seem to be unaffected by the quality of the relationship between the people concerned.

### Is ESP affected by shared genetic history?

For most of us the idea of thought transference is more credible in the case of identical twins. Despite accepting the splitting of the zygote as scientific fact it is not difficult to imagine that an original spirit might still belong to both.

An analysis of those who gave positive answers to the ESP questions throws an interesting light on this idea too.

| Type of Twin | Identical Girls | Non-Identical Girls | Identical Boys | Non-Identical Boys | Boy/ Girl |
|---|---|---|---|---|---|
| Size of sample | 157 | 80 | 29 | 20 | 62 |
| Twins report | 54 | 49 | 18 | 1 | 30 |
| Parents report | 6 | 4 | 10 | 2 | 9 |
| Total as a % | 34% | 61% | 62% | 5% | 48% |

A comparison between the genetically identical girls sample and the quite definitely genetically different boy/girl sample shows proportionally more incidents being reported by those who are not alike. As more identical men claim to have ESP than do identical girls in this sample, it would seem to be independent of their external affinity also.

The higher incidence of boy/girl pairs who reported ESP in this sample will also come as a surprise to anyone who had felt that the natural divergence of interests between boys and girls would have broken down any close ties at an early age. In fact one of the most convincing anecdotes of a strange communication between twins came not only from a boy/girl pair but from a pair who were in no way close.

### One twin's story

"My sister and I were evacuated during the war but unfortunately she was placed with a family who were much less comfortably off than the one who took me in. When we returned home she continued to feel resentful and when she grew up she became almost a recluse having nothing to do with us. She went to live on the outskirts of a village in Wales and we did not keep in touch. A few years ago I had a heart attack and was rushed to hospital. When my wife returned home late that night after visiting me she had a phone call from my sister who had had such a convincing feeling of my having been in danger that she got out of bed and walked into the village to find a phone."

This particular story seems to meet most of the usual objections which are raised on hearing tales of ESP. It seems that there was a genuine geographical distance between the twins. There also seems to have been a distance in time between their having been in contact with each other. No slight concern over her brother's high colour at their last meeting could for example have given rise to a growing anxiety which might have come to a head by coincidence on the night of his attack. The phone call too seems to have been made at such inconvenience to her that the likelihood of its having been a chance call can be ruled out.

This story, however, can also be used to illustrate some of the flaws in speculation which is almost always based on hearsay. The person reporting the facts is doing so from his point of view and not in the presence of his sister who could tell us whether she had, as was implied, left her house late at night to make her way into the village to find a phone box, or perhaps instead that she had happened to be in the phone box just because it was late at night because she was phoning for a taxi to take her home. She may have stayed there in the warm until the taxi arrived and to pass the time suddenly thought of her brother whom she had not seen for years, reminded of him by association of ideas, he having been a taxi driver earlier in his career.

Looking at all these pros and cons, it is clear that many reported experiences which appear to be the working of extra-sensory perception may be entirely coincidental. Peter Watson in his book *Twins* looks more deeply at this subject and explores an interesting theory on the subject.

Here, however, we will present what twins and their parents have reported, and let the reader come to his or her own conclusions.

Experiences which twins felt attributable to something more than mere coincidence fell into three categories. The simultaneous expression of identical thoughts, sympathetic pain and an ability to anticipate imminent contact.

### Anticipation of imminent contact

This rather grand title covers a large group who claimed that whenever they picked up the telephone to ring their twin it was invariably engaged because their twin was already on the line to them.

The other group in this category are those who claim to be able to sense when their twin is about to visit them even in situations where he or she is not expected.

"My brother, who worked as a traveller, would often drop in in passing and we never knew when he would call. One day my mother pointed out that I often seemed to know when he was about to come. I was surprised as I thought she shared this feeling but when I checked with her it seemed to be something peculiar to me alone."

### Simultaneous expression of identical speech or thought

This category included most of the everyday occurrences which twins had noticed between themselves.

"I would be thinking of a tune and he would sing it."

"We frequently make the same remark in unison using exactly the same words."

"We often answer a question that the other has not yet asked."

"While out driving one day we passed a car. I said, 'Oh that was . . . ', unable to remember the boy's name. Instantly my sister supplied it and knew who it was although she had not seen him and had no way of telling who he was. Neither of us had seen him for six years."

### Simultaneous identical written work

This section contained all those who were bitterly offended by being accused of copying at school.

"After one exam we were told to go and see the headmistress who began to tell us off for copying each other's work. When I managed to get a word in I pointed out that we had in fact been in different buildings while writing our exam papers. The teachers couldn't get over the fact that there were only a few marks between us and that in several of the written pieces we had used almost the same words."

"In RE class we were asked to illustrate our conception of life (wheel path etc.). My twin and I were sitting at opposite ends of the class and the teacher had not realised we were related, far less twins. We produced exactly the same idea—a path with branches off down to the very details of the woods and flowers by the path . . . the teacher and friends found this incredible."

"John and Peter, the identical pair of my triplet set, took an English exam at school sitting well apart, and their papers were nearly exactly the same."

### Simultaneous expression of identical taste

This section contained all those who had bought the same garment on the same day in different towns. It also contained the largest group of all who had bought each other or a parent the same card or present on a birthday. Others had bought the same pattern to make up the same dress, but the most vexing of all must have been experienced by the twins who had made an identical choice of wallpaper for their houses.

Simultaneous expressions of taste and even of words are not too difficult to explain in terms of common environment. It may well be that they happen to others but are not noted because the participants and their friends are not looking for common occurrences, whereas society creates an atmosphere in which twins and their associates around them are always keen to notch up another score on the side of ESP.

### Sympathetic pain

The situation where one twin feels the pain of the other's injury is however much less susceptible to explanation. It is also the one most frequently authenticated as doctors are often called in.

In some cases the well twin is aware of what has happened to the other and could be said to be coming out in sympathy through shock.

"Having broken my arm as a child, my sister had difficulty moving her arm without pain for a week."

"I burnt my arm and my brother was found to be struggling to use his left hand at school."

In this category must come the huge number who reported sympathetic pain, sickness, and even swelling of the abdomen during their twins' pregnancy. Almost all of those affected were aware that their twin was pregnant, but there were a few cases where pains were felt suddenly coinciding with an unexpected miscarriage or when a birth was premature. Several twins reported having undergone the same operation at the same time but in different hospitals in different towns. All of those were identical twins whose bodies would tend to have been attuned to similar biological clocks. Almost all of these instances were developmental diseases like cancer or arthritis, as opposed to diseases which attack the organism from without like cholera or measles.

"We have both had to have our left knee cap removed in different hospitals."

"We both have trouble with nerves in our neck causing pain in our backs and numbness down the left arm. She always thought it was due to her nursing and the heavy work involved but I have the same problem and have done no heavy work. The doctors say we have trapped nerves in our necks. We have never been examined by the same doctor."

But on occasion the circumstances are less prone to explanation.

"Small things—like falling over and hurting the same ankle."

"I once visited my sister and showed her a massive bruise on my leg but didn't know how it got there. She then showed me her same leg with an identical bruise, she had trapped hers in a car door."

As adults are likely to be aware of the expectation of telepathy between twins, instances taken from the experience of children might be felt to have a more authentic ring.

"I distinctly remember the feeling of sitting in the fire when I was three, but in fact it was my sister who scorched her bottom, not me."

"As babies I used to put them out in the garden in separate prams. One day I heard one of them screaming and rushed to see what had happened. He seemed perfectly all right but when I glanced at the other one I found he had been scratched in the face by a passing child with a razor blade. Despite the blood all over him he was not the one who cried."

"I had one up all night screaming with ear-ache but when the doctor examined him the next morning he could find nothing wrong. On checking his brother on the off-chance he found that he had a badly infected ear—he was as confused as I was."

An observer has sometimes been with the child who either reports knowing of something happening to their twin or can be seen to experience some unexplained pain.

"The first twin had an epileptic fit at the age of ten. The other twin was with her uncle at the time. He said 'Pop into grandma's, Mum will be a little late home from work.' The second twin replied 'She's not at work she is with Margaret—what's wrong Margaret is sick and dizzy and so am I.' Afterwards every time Margaret had a fit Janet knew."

"I was upstairs making the beds with one of the girls and a neighbour was talking to the other downstairs. The one with me was driving me mad jumping on the mattress so in the end I gave her a smack. When I came down my neighbour asked me if I had smacked Sonia, as Gemma had suddenly clapped her hand to her leg and given a yell in mid-sentence." The mother was convinced this had been an example of extrasensory perception as she explained. "Although with her sharper hearing she might have heard me giving the smack I don't see how she could have known just where it had landed."

The best documented cases of sympathetic pain are the ones which happen where twins are separated by geographical distances. Several twins in the survey were able to supply experiences of this.

"Once I was very ill with stomach pains during the week. By the weekend I was doubled up in agony so much so that my mother called the doctor. His automatic response was appendicitis. As fast as they appeared the pains disappeared on the Sunday night. On Monday morning we had a telegram to say that my brother had had acute appendicitis and had had an operation on the Sunday night. The odd thing about this was that he was in the navy at the time serving in Gibraltar."

This sort of experience, as we have seen with the smack, does not only apply to the major types of pain.

"I woke in the middle of the night with an awful cramp in my arm but just as I was going to rub it, it disappeared. I remember being rather puzzled and mentioned it next day to my sister-in-law. 'Oh,' she said, 'that would have been Donnie. The silly bloke had a shower before going to bed and forgot to take off his watch. At about three o'clock he shot up in bed saying his arm hurt and what with the heat of the shower I suppose his arm had swollen and his watch was constricting it. He was all right once he had taken it off.'"

It seems as though extrasensory experiences between twins

can include the most trivial of everyday matters. Some twins said that they were so used to this phenomenon that they took it in their stride.

"Actual incidents are hard to recall as they happen so often."

"We had similar pains when we were younger but as we grew older I just put it down to our being identical."

"At first we found it coincidental but now if we have an unexplained pain we contact each other just in case it's the other who is ill."

"It's such a nuisance as you suffer twice as much as other people—we are not ill together but we are affected if the other is ill—feel dizzy for example."

"My sister phoned me once from Canada saying, for goodness sake get along to the dentist and get your teeth seen to. I am having raging tooth-ache here and X-rays show there is nothing wrong with me!"

## Just knowing

Some twins' telepathic experiences did not involve pain but were described by them as 'just knowing'.

"He ran away from college—I felt something was wrong but didn't know what had happened till much later when Mum and Dad told me."

"My brother is a policeman and he was called to the Toxteth riots. I knew nothing about them till afterwards but remember I felt very uneasy and had the feeling that he was afraid at the time."

"Often if I feel depressed for no reason at all I wonder if it's Sandra's fault and sure enough the phone will ring and she's in trouble."

Some twins seemed to pick up the emotional mood of their twin rather than any physical pain they might have suffered.

"I was waiting for a bus to take me to college, my twin having caught the previous one, when I was overcome with misery. I sat crying on the bus. At arrival at college Hannah was waiting for me to take her home as she'd fallen down the stairs skinning her legs badly."

*One-way ESP*

It is usually assumed when ESP and twins are discussed that there will be a two-way communication. According to twins in this sample this does not appear to be the case.

"It seems that my sister is the mind-reader more than I."

"My twin does not get it from me to her at all."

"I think my twin feels more of a bond with me than I feel with her, I have experienced telepathy at times but not with my twin. She however has an uncanny knack of knowing what I am up to whether I want her to know or not. It's a sort of one-way ESP and that really bugs me."

*How does one know it's ESP?*

Echoing the twin who asked, "Am I getting a message or is it indigestion?" one cannot help but enquire just how a twin knows that what he experiences relates to his twin and not to himself. Some as we have seen did not in fact know but others came near to giving some description of what they had actually sensed.

"I just feel unwell but know it's not me."

"I know when he is ill my stomach knots up and his name is repeated to me."

"It takes the form of hearing voices—my twin calling to me in the street."

"I get restless and unable to settle to anything—the day she left her husband I was up all night though unaware of what had happened."

Although sometimes twins may feel this sort of contact between them to be a welcome confirmation of their special role as twins, most would echo the sentiments of the girl of a boy/girl pair who said,

"It makes me go cold sometimes when these things happen."

It is significant that pain, distress and disaster seem to make the waves that the sensitive pick up. No one reports a sudden access of unexplained joy which is later found to have coincided with their twin having won a million pounds. Perhaps this does in fact happen but there is not the incentive to investigate a surge of unexplained happiness as there is to find out the cause of a twinge of pain.

*The place of ESP in the study of twinship*

The comments of twins and their parents in this sample have not added greatly to our understanding of the working of extra-sensory perception but it has added something to our under-standing of its working between twins.

Psychic sensitivity appears to resemble having an ear for music, a circumstance less dependent on one's state of mind than on a particular arrangment of the hearing cells in the brain. No interference from outside short of a violent blow on the head is likely to affect one's appreciation of rhythm and tone.

From what was reported by the twins in the sample, it would appear that ESP can neither be influenced nor controlled by anything outside. Even the twins themselves felt it to be elusive. Only one out of the 132 familiar with the experience claimed to have any ability to 'use' their gift.

"As my brother is away from home (and I know this sounds stupid), if I need to contact him I just think about him and he will ring before the required time."

Single born Travers Christmas Humphreys on the other hand gave the impression that by working at it he and his wife had managed to be very much in control of their telepathy.

Discord between twins did not seem to disturb the working of ESP, and separation by distance and time seemed almost necess-ary for its manifestation.

From the down to earth accounts twins have given of their experience of this seemingly supernatural phenomenon it would seem that those involved with twins should give it no more notice than they would to any other natural attribute. Parents and teachers are sometimes unnecessarily wary of this subject and may be guilty of reading far too much into its supposed presence. Referring to it in an assessment of a twin relationship may blind the observer to what is really going on.

"I would not go so far as to say there is telepathy between them, but they are so close that they think and feel the same. I feel that in some ways they are too close, but this does not stop them from going out with lots of friends, although it does mean they think and like the same things."

The introduction of the idea of telepathy into this assessment has in fact confused the issue and clouded the observer's perception of what exactly it was about the individual twins which he had found disturbing. ESP, if it exists at all, should not be used to set twins apart into a category beyond the reach of normal estimation. Following the analogy of those who have an ear for music one should bear in mind that even infant prodigies may benefit from having their bottoms smacked from time to time.

# CHAPTER 18

# *Adolescence*

*Puberty and the physical differences*

Children's biological clocks seldom synchronise with their chronological ones. There is therefore no guarantee that twin children will reach the milestones of puberty hand in hand. Even the identical twins in the survey bore this out.

Only one-third of the twins in Britain are identical pairs and of these some pairs are more identical than others. Twins who result from the latest splitting of the zygote at the embryo stage have already spent some days of their life as one being. They are the pairs most likely to share the timing of their biological cycles. For example, the separated siamese twin girls who took part in the survey were among the few who had started menstruation on exactly the same day.

Mothers of other identical girls gave a less tidy picture. There were only two other cases of twin daughters who started their periods within twenty-four hours of each other. Four others mentioned gaps of three days to one week. The majority remembered a gap of as much as three to six months, but for some the time lag had been as long as a year. Interestingly enough, mothers of non-identical girls also told of two pairs whose periods had started on the same day, and of one set whose onset had been two weeks apart. The commonest length of time between this development in fraternal twins had been one to two years.

The longest time that any twin in the survey had had to wait to catch up with her sister was three and a half years. As the normal age for the onset of the menarche lies anywhere between the ages of ten and seventeen, this sort of gap is well within the norm and might be experienced by any pair of fraternal girls.

*Being out of step*

For some pairs being out of step in this way had put a strain on a previously happy relationship.

"Although I was the 'youngest' twin I started my periods first and I remember being acutely embarrassed about it in front of everyone—even my twin. One wants to cling to the innocence and freedom of childhood as long as possible and I wanted to be like her—not having to bother with all that grown-up nonsense and seriousness. She at the time treated me with great contempt and no sympathy whatever which made the experience nigh on unbearable. I see now that she was horrified that I had gone and started this dreadful curse that must now imminently come to her and she blamed me for it absolutely. It was, however, a fairly long time after that her periods began and she became much kinder."

The developmental difference which had caused most anguish for boy twins in the survey had not centred on the more sensitive sexual ones but on the plain question of height.

"We had big problems when at one time one was two and a half inches taller than the other—the smaller one had a more difficult adolescence."

It was bad enough to be left behind by one's classmates when their development seemed to surge forward but to be left behind by someone all the world knew to be one's twin had been a source of silent misery.

Being smaller created problems when the boy's twin was a girl. He felt it most but the girl did not enjoy it either.

"My son was much smaller and hated it. He became aggress-ive, but his behaviour improved when he eventually grew at least a head taller than his sister."

The sisters said things like,

"I never needed a rest from my brother's company till adolescence when he seemed 'younger' somehow."

*Time lags in development*

At puberty, time lags in development can not only be disconcert-ing for twins but may also provide problems for their parents.

"Penny was ten years old when she came home from school in tears because she found training for sports day uncomfortable. I told her I would take her shopping for her first bra after school. Lindsay naughtily had her giggling school friends waiting for her return"—in this case the tables were turned and, "Penny soon became the envy of all her school friends and her twin who wanted to know when she could have one."

The practicalities of providing a first bra or explaining the use of sanitary towels were easily managed. What did cause problems was the timing of the explanations about what was happening to their bodies when one twin needed to know and the other one still treated it all as an embarrassing joke.

"It was difficult to explain things to them separately as the other would feel left out," said one parent. "One was developing and needed to discuss this, whereas the other was not yet. I had to explain together because if one passed it on to the other there was a danger of possible exaggeration and confusion."

## Special facts of life for twins

Twins, in fact, do run a greater risk of getting the wrong end of the stick where their sexual development is concerned. There are two or three twin bogies to be found milling around in the great smutty stories stewpot which circulates the playgounds of independent and state schools alike.

The Mysterious Myth of Sterility is one. The Haunting Horror of Homosexuality is another.

"I can remember as quite young children that somehow we were led to believe that only one of us would be able to have children when we were married," recalled one twin. "As we got older we realised that this was not true—we both have children."

This common belief originates from old farming communities where people were familiar with the phenomena of the freemartin, a product of twinning in cattle.

It was then assumed wrongly that the same thing would happen with human offspring. A freemartin occurs when a cow gives birth to twin calves of different sexes. The female calf is sterile and odd in other ways because the male hormones from the other calf cross the placenta and enter the blood stream of the female foetus altering and distorting its development.

It is now known that the bovine twin placenta works differently from our human one and that there is no need to question the fertility of any girl because she was born a twin. Female fraternal twins are indeed quite likely to be *more* fertile than most as they stand a good chance of having inherited their mother's high fertility which accounts for their being twins in the first place!

Another myth of twin development implies a high incidence of homosexuality among identical males. It was difficult to discover the origin of this idea which actually appeared in print. Two major clinics who deal with this type of gender disphasia agreed to check their files but neither found any record of twins among their patients and none of the staff could remember having come across any evidence to support this supposition.

One of the identical male twins in the survey did acknowledge that he was attracted to members of the same sex but he went on to say that his brother was definitely heterosexual in his choice of partners. This was the same in the case of the notorious Kray twins. In his book *The Profession of Violence* published by Granada, John Pearson, their biographer, makes it quite clear that while Ronnie was attracted to other men, Reggie remained consistent in his preference for women.

The idea of a high incidence of homosexuality among identical males would seem based solely on the crude speculation of the nudge and wink brigade who prop up the bar and pass the time of day in speculation as to just how well identical twins might get to know each other. There seems to be no evidence at all that a twin is any more at risk of being affected this way than anyone else in the wider singleton population.

Sniggerers will also speculate about the degree of intimacy between boy/girl pairs. In the survey one boy went so far as to give "having to put up with snide remarks about incest" as a reason for wishing that he had never been a twin. Parents need to be aware that their children are likely to be subjected to this kind of jibe so that they may see beyond an apparently unreasonable refusal to, say, escort a sister to a school dance.

One understanding mother remembered,

"When at different senior schools they occasionally came home on the same bus but one would be upstairs and the other downstairs and they would get off at different stops. Of course that was at the adolescent stage when neither wanted to be seen with someone of the opposite sex."

The general uncertainties of adolescence are bad enough without having to put up with extra apprehensions about non-existent effects of having been born a twin. Fortunately accurate information and sympathetic understanding will clear away most fears much as the touch of a switch dispelled their night fears when they were tiny.

## Sexual awareness and the discovery of self

For some twins it was their physical imbalance at puberty which disturbed a previously comfortable partnership but for others a dawning awareness of the opposite sex fuelled a new dissatisfaction with the concept of their identity as a pair. For most girls in the survey the advent of the boyfriend had brought about a change of emphasis. The need to be seen as a single self was at odds with a passive role as partner in a pair.

"When we started getting interested in boys I wanted to be different from my sister," said one.

"Being confused was not really annoying till we were teen-agers and boys came on the scene. Then we wanted to be known individually."

Once twins had begun to explore their own identity rather than that of the pair, boyfriends were not the only ones they hoped would see them for themselves. A word of praise from a popular teacher or from the boss at work was to be coveted but where it was given in the mistaken belief that one was one's twin it would not only hurt but turn the knife in the wound.

## Being seen for one's self

All adolescents aim to be seen for themselves rather than an appendage of their parents but for a close twin the struggle is more complicated. Not only have outsiders always seen him as part of a pair but up to now he too has seen himself as "one of us". The idea of 'just me myself' can be quite difficult to grasp. The initial effort often involved an abrupt rejection of any association with one's twin and a hurried search for tangible means of emphasising this.

"I do have a terrible fear of being like her and will act very irrationally to avoid this. For example, when she had her hair cut in the same style as mine I immediately had it permed in a style I have hated ever since."

"Wanting to look different became more and more important and now (at eighteen years) I am totally paranoid about wearing anything similar to what my twin is wearing—although it is wearing off now that we are going our separate ways."

The problem of being seen for oneself is one which affects all twins who have been mentally 'paired' since birth. But the problem is obviously a more difficult one where identical pairs are concerned.

*Identity and identical dress*

To singletons the difficulty of telling one twin from the other would seem to be solved simply by their wearing different clothes, but the genetically identical twins in the survey seemed to have had genuine difficulty in perceiving this as the obvious solution. Before this discussion of adolescence it was rather difficult to produce reasons why dress should be important but at this stage the drawbacks of what has been imperceptibly acquired as a habit can be seen.

In the previous chapter we saw genetically identical twins genuinely unaware of the effect that their dual image had on the world outside. Added to that an identical twin may have a poor appreciation of his own individual visual image.

One pair of parents remembered,

"We were very puzzled by Victoria at one stage when she decared herself to be the odd one out, even suggesting that she did not belong—that we had adopted her. Since she was the mirror image of Christine, her identical twin, and not unlike her sister, this was ridiculous."

The twins in the survey provided other examples of individuals who had not seemed to be totally clear about their own visual image.

"You must understand the difficulty of not being able to recognise one's own face," one girl said.

"I turned round in the store to my cousin and said, 'Look Claire, there's Di!'—and walked straight into a mirror."

This was one of at least ten stories of this type.

What is surprising here is not that twins think that their mirror image is their twin but that that impression will often last long enough for them to gesture to it or even to start to talk with it. The last thing that seems to occur to them is that it might be a reflection of themselves.

Amram Scheinfeld may have given us a clue to the cause of this in his book *Twins and Supertwins* published in the UK by Penguin, when he tells of twin girls preparing for a party. One was overheard to say to the other,

"Stand still a minute so I can see what I look like."

Because identical twins' own image is always readily available to them outside themselves some have never had to take the trouble mentally to internalise what they look like. Their individual sense of visual identity therefore remains very vague.

This confusion of visual identity also has an effect on the concept of self.

"If I am out driving in my car," said one twin, "and I pass my sister driving her car I think—'Oh there's me' when it's really her."

This confusion can have a more serious aspect too.

"I used to get mad with Penny if she looked awful, because I felt it reflected me—that I was looking awful too."

### Identical dressing—a confirmation of twinship

In the survey, twins like those above tended to have a very highly developed sense of twinship. The external factor of being identically dressed was enjoyed as a reaffirmation of their dual identity. Long before they are able to appreciate the effect of their double entrance on outsiders, some baby twins will cry if attempts are made to dress them differently. Toilet training this pair can be a nightmare for if one wets himself the other will insist on having his (unseen) pants changed too.

By three and four years old these twins are adamant about their wish to look the same.

"They have modelled clothes in a fashion show—the poor shop owner expected them to wear two different outfits each time they walked down the cat walk—instead the audience saw too identical outfits and the show took twice as long!"

Identical dressing persists for other reasons also. Some parents who had intended to give it up after the pram stage found that any variation caused so much argument that they continued, in order to keep the peace.

"I don't think it is a desire to look alike," said one mother, "but the feeling that the other's clothes are nicer if they are different."

Parents can feel constrained by this feeling too.

"I found if I went to buy them, say a new jumper, there was always a colour I liked better and my problem would be who would I put in my second choice."

Identical dressing can also prolong the time we parents continue to enjoy the reflected glory of the "Twins how nice!" remarks from passers-by, which many of us miss once our children are not longer recognised as twins. For these reasons, both identical and non-identical twins tend to start life dressed alike. Most however, do lose the habit on the way through primary school. It is the mutual desire of some twins to continue identical dressing on into later life which points to the possibility of some deeper significance which may attach to it for them.

### Identical dressing—seen as twinship itself

In the survey, an identical girl objected to one of the optional answers to the question on dress, which was—"IF YOU DRESS ALIKE IS IT BECAUSE . . . You find it *fun* to be recognised as twins."

"I think the word 'fun' in this question is the wrong word," she wrote.

"We did not dress alike because it was 'fun' to be alike, we were the same and proud of it and we felt uncomfortable to dress differently. To wear something different was like going to school without a uniform when everybody else was in uniform and not because it was against the school rules. On the rare occasions that it did happen we felt conspicuous and unhappy."

So what did happen when they began to dress differently?

"When we finally made our decision to dress differently we went shopping separately and came back with coats made of the same material and colour but slightly different in style and felt we had been unfaithful to each other when we first wore them."

These girls had made a mutual agreement to buy different clothes so it was not to each other that they had been unfaithful. It was their 'dual identity' which had been betrayed. It became clear during the survey that for some twins identical dressing can become synonymous with the twinship itself.

Young twins will often make this mistake.

"My five-year-olds asked one day if I would buy them different clothes as they did not want to be twins any more," one mother remembers. "For two days I dressed them differently and on the third morning they wanted to go back to being twins again."

We tend to assume that when these little boys said that they did not want to *be* twins any more that what they really meant was that they did not wish to *look like* twins but it is important to make sure that young twins do in fact know that there is more than a semantic difference involved.

For some twins whose only experience had been that of being half of a matching pair, the idea of abandoning identical dress was quite frightening and seemed to invite the end of twinship. For others, however, the occasional change of style opened their eyes to new possibilities and prepared them for the day when they would branch out on their own.

"It was good to have different clothes to try and find out what it was like to be a single person. Sometimes being two was like being a shadow."

Identical dressing is undeniably a way of celebrating an enjoyment of twinship, but for twins themselves it can obscure the fact that they are 'single people' too. By adolescence, for some twins identical clothes had become identical straitjackets, preventing their development as individuals.

*Parents could have helped but most had hindered*

Unfortunately, according to this survey parents were the last to see any reason that their children should break out of this identical shell.

"It was very difficult to do anything about being dressed the same, as our parents enjoyed having the attention while we cringed," said one twin.

"My mother set great store by our appearance," said another.

"I have a horrid recollection of trudging miles to look for shoes and having to have boy's shoes in the end because they were the only ones that could be bought alike."

Similarity of dress seemed even more important to some parents than attractiveness.

"Mother would take us into a shop and say—'What have you got two of?'"

"We didn't mind being dressed alike so much but our choice was always so limited," explained one pair.

It was interesting to note also that only half these girls who were dressed alike in the survey were genetically identical pairs. The parents' insistence on dressing their fraternal daughters alike was solely inspired by the fact that they had been born as a pair.

### Branching out

Society's "Twins how nice" reaction actually becomes weaker as twins get older. Identically dressed babies are delightful, five-year-old look alikes cute, but adolescents who dress the same are slightly disturbing. Adults are suspected of doing it only for fun, and the elderly couple who still dress alike are regarded as slightly sad. A butterfly, ready to fly, who had chosen to remain in his chrysalis might inspire some similar regret.

In the survey the majority of twins said,

"At sixteen we didn't want to be dressed alike any more." Other elaborated this thought,

"When we left school we felt it was a bit childish, up till then we always wanted to be exactly the same but now we felt we had had enough of being 'images' and we wanted to branch out on our own a little bit. It wouldn't have suited us any sooner. We both agreed that adult twins dressed identically look somewhat stupid—holding on, not knowing when to let go the twin 'label'."

The word 'childish' recurred sufficiently frequently to show that the twins themselves had seen the discarding of identical dress as part of their move towards maturity. This change was not made overnight, however, and anyone trying to hurry the pace from outside would only have frozen its progress.

Even when both were in agreement the actual change was made with caution.

"At adolescence we did not want to dress the same any more but only to the extent of not wearing the same clothes at the same time—an attempt at separate identities but not too much."

*The male contribution*

Dress tended to have less significance for men. As with women, some of their common choice of clothes had to be put down to the shared taste of two people with a common genetic heritage. With men, the narrow range of garment choice had also played a part. One wife added her comment to her husband's answer on the questionnaire form, where he claimed not to dress like his brother.

"Not true," she wrote. "Only last week they both turned up with identical trousers bought at different times in different shops in different towns."

With identical twin girls this same taste had led twins living at opposite ends of the country to buy the same dress pattern and make it up in the same material

Despite this, however, many men in the survey had managed to introduce variation into their clothes and the majority fell into one of two categories; those who had stopped dressing alike in their early teens and the others who had never dressed alike or at least as one put it "not since Mothercare". It was significant, however, that even in this small sample of twenty-nine monozygotic males, three pairs in their thirties had answered 'not yet' when asked when they had stopped dressing alike, one said he changed when he got married at twenty-four and another remembered stopping only when he had begun to go out with girls.

*Finding the individual in the pair—Are you you or your twin?*
*Saying no to labels*

The men's contribution to the subject of dressing alike concentrated more on their rejection of those who had tried to circumvent its effect. Identical dressing projects the pair image and any distinguishing mark which would help outsiders to treat twins as individuals will dispel that effect. Badges, name labels, or embroidered initials had been deeply resented by more boys than girls.

"When apprentices in the same factory for a short while we had our names on our boiler suits to identify us, as foreman and workers were confused. I resented it as I thought it childish—or rather that I was being treated as a child."

In the questionnaire, the question about wearing something to help people tell them apart had been preceded by one which asked how they felt when people claimed to be unable to distinguish them, one from the other. Taken together the answers presented a strange contrast of complaints that no one took the trouble to try and a stubborn refusal on the twins' part to do anything to make it easier for those who might be willing to make the effort. Answers like,

"It bored me to hear people say they could not tell us apart because it was patently obvious that such people just couldn't be bothered to try," would be followed by statements like,

"I would have resented having to wear a badge—no, it seemed other people's problem."

The comments of other twins revealed a startling gap of misunderstanding between those who ask twins to wear a distinguishing mark so that they may treat them as individuals and the twins themselves who saw such badges as having quite the opposite effect.

"Someone once gave me a badge with my name on it and although I never resented the suggestion I never wore it—doing something like that emphasises that you are a twin and I wanted to be an individual."

This twin seemed quite blind to the fact that he was effectively preventing other people from treating him as the individual he wanted to be.

Other twins expressed the same thought.

"I think everyone is different, even identical twins, and I would have hated for us to have to act as if we were not the same as everybody else and needed to be segregated—it would have made us feel inferior."

"I detested having to 'look' different because I always saw myself as different not just in looks but in personality."

The idea of wearing badges obviously touches something deeper than is intended by the single born people who suggest it. Where labelling is done with marked insensitivity then of course one can understand this resentment.

"We had one bad experience towards the end of primary school where the headmistress made us look like fools. She marked my nose with yellow chalk. Friends laughed at us—I could not rub it off for fear of the teacher."

Happily, distinguishing twins at school is normally done with more tact than that. Sometimes a teacher can spot some difference that already exists, a wart on a finger, or the fact that only one chews his pencil. Otherwise coloured socks or hair clasps may serve. As a last resort, embroidered initials or name brooches (which are after all worn by lots of other children) will help those concerned to be sure that each child is given the specific attention that is his right as an individual. But despite this apparently worthy intention there will still be twins and parents of twins who regard any such efforts almost as a personal affront.

Surely there is something strange going on here. Few twins can give a clear objection to what they call 'labelling'. One twin suggested it was best seen as an attack on their dual identity.

"Twins have a mutual as well as an individual identity. Labelling sets them apart by their physical differences and not by their personal differences," he said.

The vast majority of identical twins in the survey had enjoyed the visible aspect of their twinship. Some said,

"When people couldn't tell us apart I felt good as it meant they recognised me and my brother as identical twins."

Others added, "When people claimed to be unable to tell us apart I felt quietly delighted."

Against this background of positive feeling it was not surprising that the question,

"Do you think your parents should have done something to help other people distinguish you one from the other?"—puzzled one identical girl twin who replied quite simply—"But why?"


## Why recognition is important

Some explanation is obviously needed although from the single born side of the fence the answer may seem to be an obvious one. The novelist, Margaret Drabble, may give us a clue as to what it is that troubles the outsider faced with a visually indistinguishable pair. In her novel *Jerusalem the Golden* she recounts her heroine's reaction to the first encounter with her friend Celelia's look-alike sister, Annunciata:

" . . . She did not like the fact of Annunciata. She resented her, she took the liberty of resenting her on Celelia's behalf. She did not like to think that Celelia was in any way thinned or dispersed or diluted by such a close resemblance; she wanted her to be unique."

Quite simply, single born people want to treat each twin as unique and in order to do so they need visual markers so that each may be entered separately in the memory. Thereafter, personality differences which emerge can be attributed to the right twin, to fill out the picture of each separate person. Recognition progresses from 'the one with the blue socks' to 'the one who wrinkles her nose when she laughs' to 'Jenny who is slow but friendly'. Without the initial hook on which to hang the other attributes a teacher may never work out that the child standing by the desk with the untidy exercise book is the same one she commended minutes before for being kind to a friend in the playground and so the positive feeling which might have tempered the subsequent telling off is not invoked.

When we are confused over the identity of the person we are talking to we try to avoid having to use their name, we also struggle to keep the conversation on neutral ground for fear of betraying an ignorance we feel might be hurtful to them. One also tries to escape from this sort of conversation as quickly as possible. Unrecognised twins will therefore receive less social contact than they would had they been clearly recognised for themselves.

The situation is complicated by the fact that this distant mode of conversation and failure to greet by name is exactly the same social signal which is used towards a person whose presence is unwelcome. In a panic to cancel this message which we know is inappropriate for the twins, we fail to take the calm slow look which might allow us to recognise them by their personality alone.

If instead of struggling stupidly we were able to focus on an 'S' for Sandra, one could warm to her immediately, instead of backing off. We would also be able to refer to her success in the play on Saturday and make the conversation much more real for her as well as for ourselves. This 'hook' that we use need not be a visible one. Where twins appreciate that the outsider's difficulty is genuine, twins who have been brought up to introduce themselves by name need never experience this problem.

My neighbour recently began to lose his sight. His wife told me that it would help him if when I stopped to chat I just said, "Hello Mike, it's Mary" before starting to speak. It was such a simple solution that it was stupid of me to have found it embarrassing at first. But now it is a habit, easy for me and a help to him. If I forget, however, I find that as he cannot 'see' me until he has recognised my voice so he does not 'hear' what I have been saying until far on into the conversation.

Parents who train their twins to introduce themselves by name will allow them to be 'seen'. In this way they will also ensure them access to the same level of social contact that is accorded to those who are single born. Social contact is important for twins as it is by observing the effect we have on others that we get to know what kind of people we ourselves are. Visually identical twins are going to get a weaker signal back from the majority of people that they meet because in their confusion they can only give a vague response, and so this vital means of outlining their individual identities may be lost to them.

". . . I know Di shared my sense that we didn't come up to the standards of the people it was important to have like you," said one identical girl.

In the survey, several comments like this revealed that quite a large proportion of identical twins suffered from a depressed self-image which may well have been the result of their having been denied this normal reassurance in their contact with others.

At adolescence in particular the discovery of the individual self should merely be a firming up of the outlines of what one already knows. But if what has been laid down over the years has all been in the context of the pair, parting for twins is going to get off to a very shaky start.

Parents nowadays have grown used to the idea that adolescence might be a time of rebellion. From the results of this survey, however, parents of twins may find that the conflict does not necessarily involve them.

"Our relationship with our sons as parents was very good during the difficult years of adolescence," wrote one set of parents. "Instead they took out all their frustrations on each other, frequently quarrelling and fighting and finding fault with each other and being hypercritical . . . This lasted from fourteen to seventeen, during which time they decided that separate universities would be a good idea. When they realised that the time to leave was approaching and that they would soon be separated for long periods their relationship improved and they parted with some regret."

According to the survey, conflict between teenage twins was very common and it was very similar to that between the single adolescent and his mother and father. Both struggles are the effort to shake off roles which have been outgrown; on the one hand the role of the submissive child and on the other that of passive partner.

The twins in the survey were asked how their relationship had fared in their teens. They were given an arbitrary age range, 5–7, 8–13, 13–17, 17–21 and over 21–marriage, and invited to tick the times when they had been friends. In isolation one could not read too much into something like this but, as in all the other parts of the questionnaire, formal answers were backed up by so much written comment that one had a wider base than numbers for the conclusions that were reached.

Despite the vagueness of the question, a very definite picture emerged. For over fifty percent of twins, adolescence had been a time of open conflict and at best a state of armed truce. The most important pattern observed, however, was that despite the almost total breakdown of some relationships in the teens almost all twins wrote that by the end of the given age span, they were getting on better than ever before. Having a twin around once one reached maturity was almost universally seen as the crowning advantage of having been born one of a pair.

"Adolescence was definitely the worst," wrote one parent but she too commented on this ensuing calm adding—"It amazes me that they have grown into such responsible adults."

Resting on this assurance that adolescent awfulness between twins will resolve itself in time perhaps we can bear to look more closely at the experience of those twins and parents for whom it had been bad.

"They seemed to hate each other," said one mother. "One needed only to pass his brother in the house for him to stick out his leg and trip him up. Not just teasing but with real malice!"

Identical girls were no better.

"From 5–7 we were mostly playing a lot together though we had the occasional fall out from 8–13, but 13–17 I can honestly say we really hated each other, sharing a bedroom especially we hated, and we argued a lot and fought. Now at 17–21 I think we get on better than ever before."

One girl suggested a reason for this adolescent discord.

"After all these years of being kind to each other it seemed as though we 'needed' to be nasty to one another and to compete for what we wanted separately."

Another thought that outside pressures had not helped.

"Between 13–17 we were always quarrelling and falling out over silly things. I seemed to be jealous of my twin as I classed myself as plain and I was fatter. This was the age when people used to compare us and we were both sensitive. I used to feel hurt and take it out on my twin."

Sometimes the struggle to adapt to new roles was cleared up in one major confrontation between the partners instead of being the cause of a succession of skirmishes.

"When I was 16 or 17 I remember asserting myself and telling my sister she could no longer control my life. It made a great difference and I think we gradually became friends after that point. It took great courage to do it—and anger and frustration spilled out that was not of her making. But it was certainly a turning point that I needed—perhaps we both needed. Till then she had manipulated me a great deal."

It seemed that some twins were able to reallocate their roles in this way because they were at the same stage of development. One twin told how she could see the justification of her twin's claim against her and altered her behaviour to relieve the situation.

"I was shocked and taken aback when she suddenly turned on me, but thinking about it I could see it was absolutely true and I began to make a conscious effort to stop seeing myself as the natural boss between us."

This twin went on to explain that she had always been the one who had been given the dinner money or the notes to take to school and so had been encouraged to think of herself as leader by her mother and others.

*Not all twins had troubles*

About half the twins in the survey had managed to establish their separate identities within the partnerships without this sort of conflict. Their growing apart had proceeded imperceptibly and for them the positive support of having a twin had come into its own.

"During puberty when life at times was rather puzzling we tried to work things out together," said one pair. Another set shared a bedroom—"where the pros and cons of parental discipline were discussed at length."

But even twins who had seen partnership to be an asset in adolescence felt the need to make a move towards some kind of separation about this time.

"I think between ourselves we were always 'you' but that other people considered us an 'us' and we felt that we had to establish that we were indeed individuals."

Following this up was not entirely easy for some.

"It's so much nicer having someone to keep you company, so I have to make a huge brave effort to go off alone—however when I do, I love the feeling of freedom and independence."

When twins had separated for a time, they began to view their partnership through different eyes.

"When I was nineteen I spent a whole year totally separated from my sister and began to develop as an individual in my own right as opposed to being a less successful double of her. Since then I've come to realise that although we're twins we are individual people with our own gifts, faults, characters, ideas and so on. Now it does not matter to me if someone prefers my twin."

*Not all twins were ready to make the move at the same time*

Sometimes one twin would set the ball rolling and wake the other up.

"This is how we got going our separate ways. My sister had a Saturday job, just mornings. I remember though when she could afford to buy her first pair of trousers and I couldn't. I was consumed with jealousy. I had never felt so strongly about anything as I did that day. I talked it over with my mother who was a great help . . . soon after I found my own Saturday job.

Our jobs meant that we spent eight hours apart from each other each week and that was the beinning of our separation . . . our split was a gradual one so I did not really notice it. However we still remain very close even today."

It is significant that this twin, who was old enough to take a Saturday job, still itemised the length of time she had apart from her twin.

### Some reactions to delayed release

Some twins who negotiated their adolescence without conflict were biding their time well aware that an opportunity for independence would be offered by the next natural break. The natural break for academic twins tends to come when they move on to further education. Some would have welcomed an opportunity to have parted sooner and so the final school years seemed filled with frustrations.

These twins tended to overstate their need to escape. Parents of two very promising boys were horrified to hear one categorically state that if the university clearing house allocated him to the same college as his brother he would refuse to go at all. Fortunately this was never put to the test but his twin remembers bewilderment that his parents had failed to understand why his twin should feel so strongly about their need to part.

Other twins whose genetic make-up had tended to channel them towards similar subjects at school chose not only different universities but different courses in order to ensure some divergence of their paths.

"Both girls gained good grades in their 'A' levels in exactly the same subjects. They both intended to do medicine but at different universities. At the last minute, however, Jane decided in an extra effort to be different to do a BSc. All went well till the middle of the first term when she rang me in tears. Jumping to the wrong conclusion I said briskly, 'Never mind dear, if you are pregnant we won't be angry, just come home and let us sort it out.' 'It's not that,' she wailed, 'it's that I've decided to do medicine after all.' "

In her desire to be different from her twin she had shied too far away from what had turned out to have been her natural bent.

Twin boys who had excelled in Classics had also reacted in this way. One chose to follow a course in Latin and Greek but the other, searching for an opposite line, chose to study Chemistry. Once again, a few terms later he too reverted to the study of ancient languages, where his original talents lay. He did, however, still cling to some element of individual difference choosing to study Anglo Saxon instead of the Greek and Latin that his brother did.

Identical twins frequently end up following the same careers even after very different beginnings. The Church of England can boast identical twin bishops. Twin surgeons, playwrights, film directors and twin teachers are not uncommon. In crafts and skills, identical twin plasterers, hairdressers and photographers also point to a mutual inheritance of talent. An older identical twin commented on these younger twins' efforts to reject similarity.

"I know now through being older—(I couldn't have written this at eighteen)—that identical twins are always the same some way or other."

Once each twin has had time to consolidate a separate personal identity however, they will discover that the acknowledgment of similar aims in life will no longer threaten their newly discovered single self.

The time needed by each twin to establish his or her self-confidence will, of course, vary. A move by one to re-establish the dual role before the other one is ready can stir up all old defensive conflicts once again.

There was a real note of panic in the voice of the twin who said,

"Recently we moved into separate flats but now my sister wants to move back again!"

Some pairs eventually managed to get it right.

"During adolescence we had fearful rows. We just had to ride out the storm and eventually at seventeen we separated. My sister went abroad and then to Birmingham to do her nursing training. After one year we decided we had matured sufficiently to be together again and shared a flat for three years before I decided to spread my wings. We are now best of friends but live in different countries."

But for other pairs a natural break did not occur to relieve the one who was ready to go and for the one who remained parting had been a painful experience.

"Any book on twins should cover the actual separation," wrote one twin who had been left behind. "From personal experience, this is one of the most traumatic times for a twin—really a typical word is grief."

Staying together does not solve the problem however. The twin who is ready to branch out may feel her new identity being stifled within the confines of the partnership.

"I know I have difficulty in being with my sister in a crowd of people and would rather leave than stay. I have been trying to overcome this sensation which I can only describe as panic and it has gradually lessened."

One twin had felt strongly enough to force the issue.

"In my late teens I emigrated to the USA. I remember feeling suffocated and perhaps burdened by her dependence on me."

The break forced on one twin by the other can be difficult, both for the twins and for the family left to support the one who remains at home. When separation has not been mutually agreed, the return of the traveller is not necessarily going to bring a happy reinstatement of the original relationship. Once again, if the one who remains at home has not taken the chance to explore her own single identity in her twin's absence, then the contrast between them on her return can be a problem.

"When twins have been as close as we were, encouraged to do the same things in school, study the same things, have the same friends and interests and then at the age of twenty-three first separate, it is very difficult to find your identity . . . I was very upset when she returned from Australia because she had changed. . . It was difficult to find that the other one who had seemed to be part of oneself was saying and doing things one did not approve of. It was as if you were being betrayed by part of yourself—I kept thinking it was not Di at all."


*At what age do most twins separate?*

Twins who had had no experience of being apart before the age of twenty-three were not rare in this sample. There were other older twins who had still not had that experience at the time they filled in their questionnaires. When asked to state the age at which they had first been away from their twin for more than two nights, several in the sample had entered the day they got married.

The average age at which twins in this survey had been separated the first time was fourteen years and six months. The higher number of twins who had been much older than this when first parting was balanced up by an almost equally large number who, because of problems at birth, were able to enter a very young age for their first separation. Fourteen years six months was a straightforward average for the rest.

The implications of this result were not immediately clear as it is not generally known at what age single born children have their first experience of fending for themselves. To check this 150 single born children in the sixth form of a suburban comprehensive school and 100 students at a sixth form college in a commercial town were asked at what age they remembered having been away from their families on their own for more than two nights. The first sample gave eight years nine months as the average age and the second nine years one month. Although both single and twin samples had only based their replies on subjective memory the difference of six and a half years represented a pretty significant gap.

This is quite a dramatic finding but it is not difficult to see how it should come about. Twins' opportunities of experiencing self-sufficiency are often delayed for quite ordinary practical reasons.

The first separations cited by most of the single students were brownie or cub camps for which they were eligible at around eight or nine. Twin children will also join brownies or cubs but because they are the same age they will attend together. For them going to camp allows some experience of separation from home but as they still have the support of their twin, this is not quite equivalent to the experience of a single child who is fending for himself.

Twins also tend to be sent together for weekends with granny not only for their mutual support but so that parents can benefit from the peace and quiet of their absence. Being able to treat one's twins as a pair is in fact so convenient that years may pass before it is noticed that although they are quite competent together they have missed out on something which is already common in the experience of their single peers.

One family had made a special effort to overcome this habit.

"All our boys, twins of six and brother of nine take turns to go singly to granny's house for weekends. This is a cause of great excitement and much packing of cases—reunion brings its excitements too!"

Laying down this pattern early in life is going to have an important effect on twins' ability to cope with separation later in their life. Parents in the survey who had put off facing the idea of separation until they had matured sufficiently to cope with the idea, had often found that they were too late to reverse a pattern which had been laid down over years. During the research for this survey, more than one parent of twins in their twenties wrote for advice on how to help their children learn to be independent of each other. Unfortunately, nothing from outside at this late stage can be made to look other than gross interference in this sort of case.

The idea of separate identity needs to be gradually nurtured from the earliest days and the view that each child is unique in himself has to be *taught* to some twins who, as we have seen, may fail to pick it up for themselves.

*Early encouragement of the sense of self*

A sense of self grows up from small beginnings. Sweeping under the bed of any five-year-old will disturb a secret cache of treasures, but if twins sleep in bunk beds where does the one above keep his secret things? The provision of a wall cabinet for the one on the top bunk may be the first thing to kindle a twin's awareness that he has a right to be treated as an individual. Small things like our practical arrangements for living can subtly reinforce or else militate against this concept. Sleeping in the same room is the norm for most young twins but this arrangement need not continue unquestioned into adolescence. The subject of shared bedrooms brought some of the strongest comment from those twins who took part in the survey.

"Up to the age of thirteen we shared a bedroom. Once in our own rooms we found things worked out better. We found we had been getting on top of each other and the slightest thing sparked us off. Silly things like when we wanted to use the mirror—we would push each other out of the way."

The timing of this move can be quite crucial however, as several parents had found.

"When we first tried our boy and girl twins in separate rooms they cried desperately for each other and it was only last year when they were six years old that we did separate them, apart from short visits to grandma. Had we not decided to part them they would have been quite happy to continue to share a room."

Other pairs had also been upset at the idea of sleeping apart and it seemed possible from the survey that confidence that one could survive the night without one's twin might be something which needs to be learned.

"Being the first girls in our huge family it seemed natural that we would share a room and as it happened, share a bed. I never slept apart from my sister till I went to university and although by that time I was twenty I remember lying there quite terrified at the idea that I should have to sleep on my own."

Parents of boy/girl pairs will be reminded from time to time to think about the possibilities of putting their twins into separate rooms, but parents of same sex twins may never have occasion to give the question a thought. It was clear from the survey that this had very little to do with the question of space. One twin wrote bitterly,

"I do resent the fact that my mother made us share a bedroom and even a bed although there was another empty room in the house."

In other cases shared rooms were effectively partitioned. It was significant that those who had found it difficult to separate when they were older had almost always shared a room. What seems to be a practical arrangement for the parents can unobtrusively reinforce the pair effect for twins as it allows no space for any ideas of self-expression to take root.

*Separation by invitation*

Parents were only able to help their children towards an early concept of individual identity if they themselves were able to resist the temptation to treat them as a pair. The pair effect works at the subconscious level and intellectual intentions of treating pre-school twins as individuals often evaporated the first time they were challenged. This had usually arrived in the guise of the party invitation addressed to only one child.

The regret that one might feel for the uninvited child in a family of spaced children was magnified into dismay when the child was a twin. Some mothers described themselves as having felt "hurt", "upset" and "sick", all fairly irrational reactions one might think. Another mother wrote,

"At twelve I don't bother any more and neither do they but when they were younger I always made sure the other one had a friend for tea. On writing this down, however, I wonder why I did it when after all there were two other children of different ages in the household. I wouldn't have made that effort if one of them had been invited to a party, so why with the twins?"

Some parents in the survey felt themselves personally involved in this situation even when their children remained unmoved.

"I was the one who was hurt—they did not seem to mind!" one remembered.

Another said, "I felt agonized but in a way very glad because I wanted them to have individual friends."

One mother was able to pin-point the source of her particular response.

"I was extremely sensitive about this . . . I think I was frightened of loving one more than the other myself—but now I am more mature I don't care who likes who as long as I love them both, which I do."

*Parties also caused a problem for outsiders*

Parents were not the only ones unsure of how to handle this situation. People inviting twins were also uncertain whether it was permissible to issue an invitation for one without the other. Asking both did not always solve the problem, for either the child tacked on because he is a twin may be left out by the two who are friends, or the twins who have been invited to play will end up playing together and exclude their host. Complications arise at all angles.

"I felt cross with the parents of the boy/girl twins in Mark's class," said a mother standing at the school gate. "We had written to ask if Brian, the boy, could come to stay overnight as he is Mark's friend at school. When I went to pick them up however, Barbara, the twin sister, made such a scene that I was terribly embarrassed. In the end another mother took pity on her and invited her to tea but surely the parents should have prepared the children for this. After all they are only six!"

By the age of ten, children in the survey could cope with individual invitations in quite a mature way.

"I was puzzled as to why he should have been asked without me but felt OK when I discovered the boy did not know my brother was a twin," said one boy.

"I was quite pleased to be left on my own," said another. "There were even times when I was glad to get rid of him!"

The problem of separate invitations is not one that lasts long, but it is important because it occurs at a stage of learning where parents' reactions give children pointers for the attitudes they will later adopt. As many as one-third of the parents in the survey had refused to allow one twin to go without the other, and turned down the invitation altogether. Another mother said,

"I persuaded them that they should both go."

A third of the parents felt that they should make it up to the one who remained behind by offering them something special.

"I usually had another child in to play . . . or took the other one out by myself."

Most mothers who felt it was up to them personally to compensate the child, found that they too had incidentally benefited from that arrangement.

"I enjoyed having one to myself sometimes. It's nice having one on his own with you."

But another had some realistic comments about this.

"It is not easy when one is invited to a party and you are left with the more difficult twin. Force yourself into a positive thinking situation, ie the more I help this child, the more his confidence will grow; the more he will be able to cope with relationships and therefore the more he will get invited out and therefore leave me in peace."

The remaining third of the sample were actually pleased to have their twins asked out individually as it was an outside confirmation that their children were being seen as the separate individuals they already knew them to be.

"I was relieved when it actually happened," said one of these mothers.

## What did the twins think?

Parents, as we have seen, tended to invest this situation with their own anxieties so it is important to find out what the twins had to say.

"I encouraged it," wrote one mother, "but they had to be persuaded that it was all right—they avoided the situation as much as possible."

Out of 300 twins, 128 had never been invited out without their twin until the advent of dating which generally heralds the end of one's childhood days.

Half the twins who had been invited out without their twin or who had not been included in an invitation addressed to their twin remembered accepting this as a natural event. Those who wrote that they had been violently jealous or "jealous till I got a bit of cake" were included in this group, on the assumption that these might well have been the natural feelings of any spaced sibling who was missing out on a treat. "Sorry he was going but not devastated," was also included here for the same reason.

The other half of the sample however remembered this situation as distressing, specifically in the context of their bonding as twins. Some of those who remained at home described their feelings in emotional terms.

"I felt lonely and unwanted," wrote one. Another said he had felt "rejected and unloved".

In this group the child who had received the invitation had been almost equally upset.

"The younger I was the more guilty I felt because it was me who was being asked out," said one.

"He wasn't happy, and I felt I had done something wrong," remembered another.

Guilt was mentioned by several twins, and apparently unreasonably it sometimes needed to be worked out later in aggression towards the one who had unwittingly caused it.

"When I returned," remembered one girl . . . "I used to wait a while then pick a quarrel with her."

Parents need to be aware of what is going on here and maybe if the uninvited child is allowed to get in a few punches the air may be cleared for both of them. As we have seen before, being treated differently in childhood tends to activate twins' need to redress the balance between them. Older twins answering on a more mature level showed their concern that the situation be balanced too.

"I felt pleased she was going out on her own and hoped she would not brood too much on my not having been asked."

And for one pair it worked.

"She convinced me that she did not mind so I was able to enjoy myself."

A small group, five percent, remembered their main dislike of separate invitations principally in terms of a fear of separation.

"I would rather not go than go without him," said one.

"If I was asked on my own I was nervous," said another. The habit of being together had become supportive, but later on it proved a drawback for some.

"I found when I reached thirteen or fourteen I didn't want to go out socially without my twin because she used to do all the talking and I felt at a loss and sort of incomplete without her. However, once I made this break I found myself enjoying life far more as a complete individual and friends commented that I was far more talkative when my twin wasn't there."

Although it is clear that different children will react in different ways to the suggestion that they attend a party on their own, this seems to be one of the first areas where parents' attitudes can help their twins to see themselves as 'complete individuals' before they reach their teens.

### Where separation is not a matter of choice

The minor separation of twins asked individually to a party is still in the hands of their parents but in this sample fifteen percent of twins had been separated by hospital admission, before they were seven years old. Society's aversion to the idea of parting young twins probably accounts for the fact that the sick child had frequently been encouraged by hospitals to bring his twin along too. In some cases medical staff showed more interest in their twinship than did their parents.

"One of my sons had to have a hole in the heart operation.

When the doctors heard he was a twin they wondered whether his brother's presence might aid his recovery—they absolutely ignored each other!"

Despite this example, however, there was sufficient evidence in the survey that admission to hospital had a dramatic effect where children were twins.

"When we knew Daren would have to go into hospital for a minor operation we were so busy preparing him for the experience, taking pains to explain what was going to happen that unwittingly we were neglecting Shaun. We didn't realise that it was just as upsetting for him. (He was going to stay with his aunt while I was in hospital with his twin.) He reacted by drawing attention to himself in every way—particularly by being rude and disobedient so he kept getting told off. Luckily we realised that his behaviour had changed and we quickly changed our attitude and gave him the attention he needed. The separation was only for three nights in the end but it was devastating for them. Had I realised how it would affect them I think I would have tried to take Shaun as well—at least to show him where Daren was."

Here, once again, the child most deeply affected by what is about to happen was not the one one might have supposed. Those twins in the survey who had been the patients in the hospital did not remember separation from their twin as having been a very great issue at that time.

"I was four years old," said one. "I never had time to feel lonely. It was a new experience."

"I had my tonsils out, I was elated. I felt I had grown up and it was my biggest adventure for years. My sister was most resentful."

It was the child who remained at home who was most affected by the absence of his twin and by the disruption of their normal routine.

"At six years old my sister had to go into hospital. It was very odd wondering what had happened to her. I was frightened for her, and for myself without her," said one.

"I felt very strange as though part of me was lost," wrote another.

Many of these children associated their sense of loss with specific practical situations.

"At ten years old my sister had to go into hospital. I felt worried, cut off, having to cope, eg having to prepare my own tea."

"I was mainly worried about having to go to school on my own," said another.

And once again, having to sleep alone had been a difficult experience at what was already a worrying time.

"At seven I remember feeling scared. I had never slept alone before. I had always shared a room with John up till then."

Feeling 'cut off and lonely' was a phrase that recurred again and again, evoking a picture of anxious parents rushing off to visit the hospital and forgetting to give the child at home an explanation of what was happening to the one who was sick. One twin went so far as to say that his mother's fleeting home visits at that time had left him convinced that she did not love him any more.

Children being both realistic and resilient however, did not confine their feelings to those which might be considered appropriately soulful for the occasion.

"I wished I were ill so I could get the attention," said one twin expressing something others had also felt. Genuine concern and fear for one's twin did not prevent some ambivalence about his being ill.

"I remember wanting him to get well and not to die, and sometimes irritation that he was such a weakling that he caught everything."

Most of our feelings about suffering and sickness are contradictory and twins who are very close may need help to recognise that such thoughts are permissible.

## Those who over-react will also need help

Because they are the same age and are likely to be playing together twins, more than other siblings, are likely to be together when an accident occurs. Parents in the survey found that the uninjured child was often the one to be the most upset.

"Shyrly was hysterical when Morag put a knitting needle through her hand. Morag did not even cry."

When a parent is occupied with the injured child at the scene of an accident it would seem wise to ask another adult to check on the well twin and if necessary to treat him or her for shock.

The over-reaction that has physical symptoms is more easily dealt with than those which have emotional undertones.

"I felt guilty that it wasn't me," said several twins.

In the case of serious and painful illness, parents will frequently have felt this too. It is a mistake to believe that we are protecting children by keeping them in the dark about anxiety and suffering where they are personally involved. All that does is to exclude them from the comfort of discussion which we would normally extend to an adult in a similar situation.

Sharing with the child the fact that parents sometimes feel guilty too, and explaining that guilty feelings often come as part of our being sad, may allow both adult and child to benefit from knowing that they are not alone with their thoughts.

Despite the trauma associated with hospital admissions for some twins, these separations gave these children their first experience of coping on their own without their twin. There was an interesting follow-up to this in the case of at least one pair.

"When growing up as an identical twin, no one could tell us apart. We were in the same class through primary school and as children we were only ever invited out together."

At the age of ten this girl's reaction to her twin's admission to hospital with scarlet fever was not surprising.

"I cried all the time. I felt very lost as though half of me was somewhere else. I did not feel right till she was home again."

But only one year later this is the twin who said,

"My sister went to a different school because she took a scholarship exam equivalent to the eleven plus. Although I was on an equal level with her and teachers and parents were very annoyed about it I would not take it as I saw it as an escape from being 'the twins'."

It is not too fanciful to surmise that the break that these girls had experienced while one was away recovering from scarlet fever had introduced them both to the idea of independent identity. Nor did this break destroy their relationship as twins as twenty years later they wrote,

"Now that we are both married and living apart we are the closest friends and get on smashing."

One would hope that a twin's first experience of separation would be less drastic than an admission to hospital. But even in these adverse circumstances the opportunity of discovering themselves as individuals can be a positive thing. Doctors and nurses respond to the sick child in her own right and at home the other can explore the joys of having the bedroom to herself.

In the survey the pattern of twins' responses to these examples of early separation tended to support the idea that a gradual planned introduction to some measure of independence over the fairly calm days of childhood could do much to prevent identity crises for twins in their teens.

Those who arrived at adolescence on similar but parallel paths, weathered their storms better than those who had approached it following an identical path, from which they then had to struggle to diverge.

# CHAPTER 19

# Changing partners

## Adolescent dating

A twinship which has serenely survived physical separations may still be seriously threatened by the introduction of a third party.

When the Beverley sisters had a hit with the song 'Sisters', the fact that they were identical twins with a look-alike sister only added visual impact to the confusion of loyalties that the words express. Any man who comes between sisters who are twins or any sister who comes between her twin and her twin's chosen man, better watch out!

## Parents' Apprehensions

Parents of younger twins in the survey expressed apprehension for the future problems that adolescent dating might present for their twins. Recurring nightmares seemed to feature either one twin as more popular than the other, or both in competition for the same potential partner. Those whose twins were already in their teens were also concerned.

"We have a boyfriend problem at the moment in that Christine has only to lift her little finger and they come running whilst Fiona finds it difficult to have a regular boyfriend. I have always said, 'treat them like individuals' so perhaps it worries me more than it worries them, but I do feel Christine should hand over some of her 'spares'!"

## When one twin was more popular than the other

The twins in the survey could have reassured their parents on this subject. The reaction of the twin without the boyfriend for example was not always jealousy. Often, surprisingly, the new partner was welcomed with relief as someone who could take over in the supportive role.

"Sandra now has a steady boyfriend whereas I don't. I don't resent their closeness, in fact I am glad she has found someone else to confide in now that I am not at home, as I feel that such a relationship is important for us who have always had someone whom we can trust implicitly."

The relationship with a boyfriend often seemed to take over smoothly where a natural break had occurred for the twins.

"I did not feel the parting was such a big thing after all, as I had a steady boyfriend at the time," wrote one girl of her twin's departure from home.

Even when a boyfriend had been resented, twins had felt that having been pushed into going their own way might not have been such a bad thing after all.

". . . And then she met her future husband and I didn't see a lot of her. I resented him for spending so much time with her—I had to get friendly with another girl and get a boyfriend. This was when we actually began to go our separate ways and for the first time our friends were entirely different groups. I was unhappy for a while not having much confidence in myself but I knew it was only me who could get it any better."

As in other situations it was not only the twin appearing to be least successful socially who reacted to the situation. The first twin to have a boyfriend was often uncomfortable to be in this position of advantage over her twin.

"I would flirt terribly with any boyfriend I brought home to show that I had a boyfriend and she had not. I knew it was mean but I just couldn't help it," wrote one girl.

This is reminiscent of the reaction of the twin who picked a quarrel after returning from the party to which only she had been asked. Contrary to expectation this is the twin who needs the explanations and support, the other, though lacking a boyfriend, is probably well insulated for the moment by a self-righteous indignation at her sister's patently bad behaviour.

Having access to the twins' point of view on these matters clarified areas where help might be welcome and indicated others where parents could perhaps turn a blind eye.

*When both twins were attracted to the same potential partner*

As this was one of the specific worries expressed by parents, twins were asked if it had ever happened to them.

The answers can be represented in a table:

| Type of Twin | Identical Girls | Non-Identical Girls | Identical Boys | Non-Identical Boys |
|---|---|---|---|---|
| Yes, attracted to the same person | 38 | 14 | 14 | 2 |
| No, not attracted to the same person | 40 | 25 | 4 | 6 |

Being attracted to the same person is a possible hazard of twinship but according to these figures it does not seem to be an inevitable corollary, even for those who are genetically identical.

Being attracted to the same potential partner is, of course, not so terrible. What matters is how one handles the competition.

*May the best man win*

The majority who admitted to having had this problem said they had waited to see what the object of their affection would do.

"The girl would sort it out," or "We waited to see what the boy would do."

There were in fact only four twins who felt that this had presented them with serious difficulties.

"This did cause problems," said one, "I invariably lost."

Another remembered, "We had great jealousy when a boy we both fancied took one of us out. It was a strain on our relationship and caused trouble."

*Prevention was better than cure—the couple effect in action*

Many twins had in fact anticipated this problem and had already laid down their own unwritten rules to deal with it.

"We said, 'If she likes him then I will not'," said some girls.

"Being attracted to the same girl never caused a clash—we arranged it," said the boys.

Sometimes the arrangement was on a conscious level.

"We had a sort of unspoken recognition of each other's 'types'.

I would be at a party and notice someone coming in and begin to think, 'Oh, he's rather nice' but then I'd almost immediately stop myself if I noticed he was one of 'hers' rather than one of 'mine'."

Some were only conscious that they had had such a defence when they looked back.

"We were never attracted to the same boy, maybe it was an unconscious safety valve not to hurt the other twin—by picking different boyfriends."

### Something more difficult

Most twins in the sample found direct competition plain sailing when compared with the problems of dealing with a new partner who dropped one twin in order to date the other.

"Once a boyfriend of mine decided he was in love with my sister and wrote to her, so she politely told him to get lost, not because she disliked him but because she would not hurt my feelings."

Earlier on in the dating game, sharing a boyfriend or girlfriend was not uncommon.

"At one time when we were ten or eleven we did share a 'boyfriend'—a situation which suited us very well at that time."

Once they grew older however and relationships were more serious, most twins shied away from this situation.

"We always made it a rule that we never went out with the ex-boyfriend of our twin."

Keeping to this rule seems to have been an exercise of far-sighted common sense.

"I went out with one boyfriend first then he decided he was not for me. Although I got on quite well with him I broke it off. He then went out with my sister and I have a feeling that she may have felt second best. Even when they were married, she seemed jealous though I never gave her cause. They had three children and then separated—I hope my sister does not think I contributed in any way to the break up."

### The pair—a problem for partners

Most girl twins were keenly aware of the problem their twinship presented to prospective boyfriends.

The advantages of being able to arrive at a party together could be cancelled out by the fact that they were then seen as inseparable.

"As teenagers our closeness prevented us from having any boyfriends—they were either put off by it or had difficulty in choosing between us."

And once a boyfriend was found, maintaining a three-way relationship was difficult.

"Boyfriends sometimes resented us being twins. A boyfriend of mine positively disliked Ann and was often rude to her which made me very angry—I think it may have been because he was jealous of her and that I would want to go places with her rather than with him."

*Identical and look-alike twins*

Sometimes the boy would try another tack.

"One boy liked us both and we both liked him and he sensed that one would be upset if he went out with the other so he tended to alternate his affection. This annoyed me as I could never see how somebody could like us both when we were so different."

In general, however, the twins themselves successfully stage-managed their admirers.

"My husband had originally asked my sister out in the first place, but as I had fancied him for weeks and he knew both of us just as well, but remembered my sister's name more easily—(also she was chattier not being emotionally involved)—we decided I should go, and after spending the whole night worrying if I had done the right thing it worked out in the end—he didn't seem to mind at all and didn't feel deceived."

Visually indistinguishable pairs who had interchanged with each other's boyfriends for fun, however, very quickly found that the boys did mind and playing tricks died out as soon as their relationships began to enter a serious phase.

*Some pointers for parents*

Although older twins had found their pairing to have been a drawback, younger ones had sometimes found it to be a help.

"Boys usually went out in pairs and we managed on many occasions to be a foursome."

The same applied to the boys.

"My brother and I went round with two girls who were friends."

This is perhaps the only time a parent might offer a suggestion. If 'going out' is still an expression of independence from home rather than a search for a serious partner the more outgoing twin of the pair might be quite happy to fix a foursome by asking her sister to partner 'one of her spares', but it will only work if the twins are happy too.

"When we started going out with boys my mother wouldn't let one go out without the other. Poor Rachel had to come along and play gooseberry, I was going out with somebody who lived a good bit away and his mother had invited me down for the weekend. I couldn't believe my ears when my mother said, 'You are taking Rachel with you too'."

### Dating and the boy/girl pair

When it comes to dating, boy/girl pairs are not in competition for the same partners and indeed their twinship may even bring them the added bonus of a constant supply of contacts with the opposite sex.

"As we gained friends we gained two-fold," said one of the girls. "(I gained all of his and he gained all of mine). I think this helped me in later life with male friendships. I am still more at ease with men than I am with women."

For the boy/girl pairs in the survey, the joint discos of their teens had been much more successful than the joint parties of their childhood, and in adolescence many found mutual support in each other—"my brother would often discuss his girlfriends and would confide in me more than he would in our parents."

Quite unexpectedly however, two problems had arisen for this particular pair.

"I think having constantly shared a boy's life may have taken the 'glamour' from my thinking about the opposite sex when other girls were reaching the age of adolescent discovery," said one girl.

Parents also wondered whether having been so close to a

brother might have delayed the awakening interest in the opposite sex, so that daughters missed out in making the practice relationships of adolescence.

"I feel that because Yvonne had a twin brother she was not interested in boys before she went to university, then she fell madly in love with the first man she met. This did worry me. Her twin brother had had girlfriends from the age of sixteen years."

Girls felt the influence of their twin brothers in other ways too.

"In adolescence I felt he had an off-putting effect on boys. He was dog-in-the-manger about them and deadly suspicious of their motives. He was always uneasy with them."

This proprietorial attitude of twin brothers was referred to again and again by their sisters in the survey. Seeking a twin's approval for one's choice of partner was mentioned by other types of twins but more from a concern that all relationships should be in harmony than as a request for permission to embark on the relationship at all.

A non-identical girl pair said,

"We saw the faults in each other's boyfriends and told each other so. We really only wanted the best for each other, looking back on it."

The motives of boys from boy/girl pairs seemed to be somewhat different.

"I do remember feeling jealous when she went out with boyfriends for any period of time between 16–20," said one twin brother. "I think this was possibly more because I knew the boys before she did and wasn't particularly keen on them. Her husband was also know to me before my sister but I always got on with him and still do."

A sharp reaction to a twin's choice of partner was not confined to the boys.

"I felt very jealous when he got engaged," one girl remembered, "but gradually I got to like his wife."

Looking back, parents of boy/girl twins had this comment to make.

"We were not ready for the amazing interest shown when they began to have boyfriends and girlfriends. It seemed to be the first time any really jealous feelings were shown. They are still—at twenty-one, very critical of friends of the other—with the boy being slightly nose put out of joint."

This particular pair had two other brothers so we can take it that these parents were commenting on something they had found to be specific to their twins.

## Marriage—but twins are already a pair

Adolescent dating is only the trailer for the big film—adult emotional involvement and full commitment. The discovery of another individual whose personality complements their own marks for most people the highest point of human fulfilment. If, however, such a partner were already to hand would there be the same incentive to go and search for another?

In the mid-nineteenth century, Sir Francis Galton commented on what seemed to be a tendency for twins to marry less frequently than their contemporaries. He suggested at the time that this might be because twins were less fertile than other people. Some years later, Rene Zazzo also noticed this trend but questioned the logic of Galton's comment on fertility. Sexual attraction, as he pointed out, has nothing to do with one's ability to have children—something that sadly many childless couples could confirm. Zazzo felt it far more likely that any reluctance to get married would be related to the fact that twins were already a pair.

Searching for some data he scanned the records of births and deaths for one of the districts of Paris. Here he found that 16% of all males and 26% of all females had remained single. Of the twins in this sample, 15% of the males in opposite sex twins and 46% of the females in opposite sex sets had remained unmarried. Among identical pairs, 25% of males and 47% of females had remained single.

Figures like these tend to raise more questions than they answer but they do serve as a useful introduction to the idea that entering the partnership of marriage may raise special complications for those who are already half of a pair.

One of the girls in the survey unwittingly put Zazzo's ideas into words.

"I think it unlikely that I will marry. Having a close companion already I don't have to spend my whole life looking for another soul mate."

This was not, of course, the view of all twins. An identical male pair felt just the opposite to be the case.

"Having been born a twin and enjoyed a partnership, it was only natural that once we became separated in our different jobs we found another partner by getting married."

### Twins were quite likely to marry twins

The next best thing to remaining with one's twin seemed to be to marry someone else who had a first-hand knowledge of twinship.

"Whilst at university, Cathy married another identical twin!" Many of the identical twins in the survey had married other identical twins and quite often identical pairs married the partners of another identical pair.

We are not particularly surprised when two doctors, two computer programmers, or two hairdressers marry each other. Twins not only share their common experience of being paired but often feel that only another twin can really understand their dual identity.

### Twins who married non-twins

After a lifetime of sharing, communication between twins can achieve a sophisticated level. A journalist describing the late President Kennedy and his brother Bobby as 'having devised a private talk of elipse and intuition, finishing each other's sentences and even interrupting to finish each other's thoughts" might have been commenting on a conversation between close twins.

A new relationship has to progress through several levels before it can match this and if one party is unaware that this is a skill which has been acquired early in life, both parties can end up confused. Several twins in the survey remembered their bewilderment at first.

"In marriage," said one twin, "there is a disappointment because you expect to be understood, which one is used to, and this can be a bit of a shock."

In more than one case it created sufficient difficulty to destroy the relationship.

"I could not understand it when I got married. Here was someone I loved and yet we were just not on the same wave length. I had not been used to having to explain to my twin why I decided to do something. She had always understood without my putting it into words. The crunch really came when I accepted an invitation for us to go out with some neighbours and my husband refused to go. I said I thought he would have wanted to go but he said that was just it, I had just thought, I had not asked him."

This marriage did not last and though there were probably faults on both sides, the wife felt that her twinship had not prepared her for this way of relating to someone else. She had not realised that there would be work to be done building up the relationship before assumptions of understanding could be made.

*Transition presented other problems too*

Several other twins related the problems they experienced in the early days of marriage directly to their having grown up as part of a pair.

"Compared with twinship, the marriage relationship was not a close one," wrote one twin. "It required more effort because there was not the same telepathy—the words and actions normally taken for granted required explanations all the time."

Expectations were different too.

"You tend to expect a much closer unity with your spouse and put more demands on that person than would normally be expected."

"When I married—even though I was very happy I became 'lonely' and depressed, being only half a person. Only years later did I realise that it was due to the fact that I had missed a constant companion—as I married an only child there came a definite realisation that I had to stop thinking in 'twos' and return to being a 'one'."

Most twins in the survey began their comments on marriage with the phrase, "At first I found it hard to adjust . . ." but happily the majority went on to say that their having had to make allowances had actually enriched the new relationship for them, even if only in practical terms.

"We talk more because we do not assume that we think alike as my sister and I did."

Those who had persevered found in the end that as the marriage matured it compared quite favourably with twinship. One twin felt she could put her finger on why this might be.

"With your husband you are both equal partners, dependent on each other but for different reasons, both giving and taking. Twins are trying to take out of each other the same things that they both need."


## The end of an era

As they mature at similar rates and move in the same social circles, many twins will marry about the same time. Several pairs in the survey had had a double wedding but in the majority of cases one married first and left the other at home. The pattern of the remaining twin's reaction related directly to the point they had reached in their adjustment to life as a pair.

Many were able to say,

"I was not unduly concerned when my twin got married as by that time our relationship had established itself into its distant routine."

But some twins were taken completely by surprise by their shock and emotional response on the wedding day itself. Although they had known in their heads for months what was about to take place, the actual ceremony seemed to spark an emotional crisis.

One girl who said, "I made a terrible fuss at his wedding—(needless to say I am ashamed to admit it now)," added, "The funny thing is that I would not have said that I felt any more for my twin than for my other brothers and sisters."

Others had reacted physically:

"In the church when the minister was marrying us she started to shake uncontrollably, felt claustrophobic, and wanted to scream to stop the whole proceedings . . ."

One might expect a sister to cry but one twin said,

"It was a strange sort of crying that I couldn't stop as though it was the end of it all."

The pain that they shared seemed to be a feeling of being

abandoned alone in a world where up to now they had been, if not physically then at least 'mentally', accompanied.

One mother said, "She thought this was their parting and that there would be no more sharing of secrets."

Fortunately it was not long before most twins realised that it takes more than marriage to sever the twin bond.

"I was married first and was upset for days because I had never before considered that the togetherness of being a twin could be over. Fortunately it actually made my twin and me closer."

### Panic adjustments

Not all twins waited long enough to discover this however. Some twins tried to cling to the old relationship and only prolonged their pain.

"After my sister left to get married I felt like an only child at home and hated it. I used to stay with my sister and her husband for a week every year or at weekends but the partings at the end of these stays were worse for me—she had a different life to see her through."

Others had catapulted themselves into unsuitable marriages rather like rejected lovers marrying 'on the rebound'. The boys of the boy/girl pairs in the survey had been the most likely to do this.

"My brother had left home to go to sea in his teens and had been away for years when I got married. He turned up before the wedding and seemed very up-tight. 'You remember,' he said, 'if he ever lays a hand on you he'll have me to reckon with!' I was quite taken aback at the very idea of my husband ever doing such a thing. After the wedding he went back to sea but in a few weeks we heard he had married a girl he had just met. It didn't last and after the divorce my mother asked him why he had ever married her. I was puzzled by his reply, 'Well, Jenny got married and I felt no one wanted me any more.' I had had no idea that his feelings had run so deep."

And for some the sentimental pressure of a double wedding had clouded their motive for marriage.

"Stewart and I picked the date and Judy said could she get married on that day too as she did not want me to beat her . . . Sadly six weeks later it was all over and they were divorced."

*Some positive results*

Not everyone had found the marriage of their twin traumatic. Some had not only been happy for them but had seen positive benefit in it for themselves.

"When I heard my twin was to be married I felt happy for her but I also felt that I too was about to start a new life and was filled with an eagerness to get on with it."

The degree of distance marriage introduced between some pairs had sometimes also proved to be the best thing for all concerned.

"Our son had always been very aggressive, especially when his sister did better, was taller, and so on . . . he has matured so much in the last two and a half years since he married and a lot of his aggressiveness has gone." Marriage finally gave this twin space for his own development so that he could now meet his sister on equal terms.

*Finding the balance*

Once twins were maried they often had to struggle to strike a good balance between the two relationships.

"I worried that my motives were honest," wrote one twin. "Had I taken the right step? Was I putting my husband in my twin's place because I resented her?—all nonsense but on and on I questioned."

Identical twins seem particularly affected.

"A concern for my sister will override a concern for my husband. He has always tried to understand this and I know sometimes he feels jealous and then I feel hurt that he should try to come between us. I want them to be exactly the same. It is a very complex feeling. My sister married an identical twin and he understands this—so I feel a very special relationship with him."

Sometimes the strength of the twin relationship would break through all the intellectual reasoning.

"It is not a competition to be the most important person in my life . . . There will always be room for both relationships to thrive together but separately—I can't go for more than a few days without seeing my sister."

But sometimes a single event served to highlight how the status of the old relationship had changed.

"When I went into hospital to have my first child, they allowed husbands only into the ward. My sister did not realise this and when she was turned away it was the first time she felt excluded and she was very upset."

### Marriage partners' reaction to twinship

It was not only identical twins who could be seen as a threat by marriage partners. The girl of a boy/girl pair wrote,

"It was difficult to explain my need to see my brother often and to share things with him. It is a different kind of closeness with a twin and it took a while for me to show my husband he had nothing to fear."

One wife had written her own observations on her husband's form.

"People ask me if I feel left out because my husband and his twin are so close. I honestly say that I have never felt excluded, in fact my reaction is 'It's great—like being married to two husbands . . .' I have never experienced any relationship as close as theirs . . . it brings a lump to my throat the way my husband automatically puts his twin brother first in feelings, work, finance, in fact everything."

But not every marriage partner found it so easy to live with. A male twin remembered,

"Neither my ex-wife nor my twin's wife could understand why we wanted to be together."

Male twins in general tended to feel that life was like that and wives should just learn to put up with it but female twins seemed more ready to try not to exclude their husbands.

"He was resentful of my sister's importance to me . . . it made me all the more determined to show he was not left out."

### Conclusion

Some twins were able to bring the advantages of having grown up as a pair into their marriage. Even a difficult twin relationship had had its contribution to make.

"I was used to being aware when tensions were building up as I had never got on with my twin."

Once the transition had been made and the previous relationship had been found to be still intact, many twins felt that this was the time when the real benefits of twinship could be enjoyed.

"My twin is my past, we share so many memories," said one girl, "but my husband is my future."

Once they had managed to sort them out, most single born people would envy twins their access to two experiences of partnership.

# CHAPTER 20

# Standing alone

It is not surprising that a study like this should linger longest over situations that involve both twins. It was, for example, much easier to see the influence of one twin on the other in the same class at school, but the mutual influence of pairs may be measured in another way; by observation of one who has been left alone.

Twins do die, and the reaction of the surviving partner is not always the same. One elderly lady wrote of her loss following the not-unexpected recent death of her sister.

"It is very hard to live without her, almost impossible emotionally, and very lonely."

Referring to the original siamese twins, she went on,

"I don't think Chang would really have enjoyed the last part of his life without Eng. He would have felt draughty down one side, and probably more afraid than with his brother, who though hell to live with because of his drinking problem, was in fact his life."

Those who have suffered the loss of a marriage partner or even a close friend may also feel this 'draught down one side', and this beautiful expression of grief for a well-loved sister would in fact have applied equally had they not been twins.

In middle life, however, the unexpected loss of a twin will sometimes trigger a recognisable pair response which seems to depend entirely on what stage of maturity the previous relationship had reached.

Norris McWhirter, co-author of the *Guinness Book of Records* suffered the sudden tragic loss of his identical brother when he was assassinated. In his book *Ross, the story of a shared life*, he tells of his thoughts immediately after having had to identify the body.

"As I was being driven back through the road block in a policeman's sports car with my head under a blanket, I felt that I was about to be re-born—not as half a person but as a double person."

This is a different reaction to that of the twin who 'felt a draught'. Recent research seems to indicate that the death of a twin may precipitate positive personal change in the survivor.

"My husband has been working with a chap whose twin committed suicide two years ago—the survivor said he felt terrible for about eighteen months and then pulled himself together—and after having been an intellectual layabout for years, he is a keep fit fanatic now and a mad cyclist . . ."

The sudden death of a close friend, or of someone within one's own family, can often stop us in our tracks and shock us into taking stock of our own lives. The reaction of a twin may be something more. Those from a pair who have shared out the various social roles of their dual identity may find that rounding up a new 'whole' identity for themselves involves taking on those things previously considered the province of their twin. A passive twin may become more active and an assertive one may become more considerate. Where twins have been in business together the survivor may find he has to take over some of his partner's work but observers will often find that in idiosyncrasy and attitude he also seems to have taken over from the one who is gone.

Trees planted close together will accommodate each other's growth so that in silhouette they look like only one. If one tree then falls in a storm the remaining one will eventually stretch its cramped branches into the vacant space and fill the gap. Some surviving twins will change and appear to incorporate the characteristics of their partner as they go on to develop on the draughty side.

But if the roots of close planted trees have become entwined, the fall of one will be a life threatening event for the other. Close inter-dependence can have a doubly tragic effect, as in the case of one twin who followed her sister's example by taking her own life as long as six years after her twin had died.

Their mother said,

"In the course of talking about my grief to my doctor, he said that when one twin committed suicide, the other is always at risk. Why were we not told this?"

In the course of my own work with twins there have been

insufficient examples to confirm this as a pattern but quite a sufficient number to prompt a strong suggestion that the surviving twin in the case of suicide should always be offered professional help.

Up to this point, the survey has seemed to give tentative support to the suggestion that twins will benefit from some early experience of separation and even conscious training for independence. The reaction of twins who had been left to carry on alone would seem to endorse that.

## Conclusion

Research results are often disappointingly banal, merely seeming to underline what one thought to be the case before any research was done.

In retrospect, the problems we have looked at may have seemed trivial. Some may feel cheated that twins turned out to be less extraordinary than they had hoped, and that the few areas of doubt can be easily resolved. As in all matters of childcare, however, the easy solution on paper is difficult to apply in practice.

"My experience has told me if possible it would be much kinder in the long run to encourage twins to have different friends etc. much earlier in life, not to depend on each other so much . . . but this is easier said than done. Mine have done everything together since being born and both were very upset when they parted at twenty-three years."

But because this survey has been able to show some of the connections between early experience and the development of later attitudes, parents of young twins can be forewarned. Because people have allowed their stories to be told we can now relate cause and effect.

One mother was rather sad to write,

"I feel out of their little world. They come straight home from school, go straight to their room and natter, appear for meals and disappear again—as though, because they have each other, that is all that matters—they seem so close it is uncanny," but earlier in the questionnaire this was the mother who wrote,

"I find myself getting upset if they are not invited out together, or if one goes somewhere without the other. I feel they should be together all the time although I know one day they will have to be separated . . ."

No one seems to be immune from the pair effect. It can gain a stranglehold on the most sensible parents' common sense.

Once aware of its danger, helping twin children achieve a balance between the supportive warmth of their dual identity and the confidence which comes from self-reliance should be the aim of all who are involved with twins. One identical girl pointed the way when she said,

"You can enjoy being a twin once you know how to be your own person."